Shakespeare and the Problem of Meaning

Shakespeare
and the Problem of
Meaning

Norman Rabkin

The University of Chicago Press

Chicago and London

The University of Chicago Press, Chicago 60637
The University of Chicago Press, Ltd., London

© 1981 by The University of Chicago
All rights reserved. Published 1981
Printed in the United States of America
85 84 83 82 81   5 4 3 2 1

Library of Congress Cataloging in Publication Data

Rabkin, Norman.
  Shakespeare and the problem of meaning.

  Includes bibliographical references and index.
  1. Shakespeare, William, 1564–1616—Criticism
and interpretation—History—20th century.
I. Title.
PR2969.R3   822.3'3   80–18538
ISBN 0–226–70177–8

NORMAN RABKIN, professor of English at the
University of California, Berkeley, is the author of
Shakespeare and the Common Understanding and
numerous articles on English Renaissance drama.

To the Memory of C. L. Barber

Contents

Preface

This small book has been some ten years in the making. It began when Eugene M. Waith invited me to address a paper on the state of Shakespeare criticism to the World Shakespeare Congress in Vancouver at the beginning of the seventies, a time when it still seemed necessary to decry the ubiquitous critical tendency to explicate meanings. In the decade in which I have been obsessed with the problem, the critical scene, like everything else, has turned upside down, and it now seems even more necessary to defend the very notion that literature—or anything—can be said to have meaning.

My book has thus grown through strenuous debate with myself as well as with others. Only its author knows how truly it owes its existence to the encouragement, intellectual stimulation, and generosity of friends who have discussed its ideas and criticized its early versions. For kindnesses large and small I take this opportunity to thank Janet Adelman, John F. Andrews, Herschel Baker, John Bean, David M. Bevington, Stephen Booth, Stanley Cavell, Robert W. Clements, Stephen Greenblatt, John Hollander, Coppélia Kahn, Elaine Kalmar, Juliet McGrath, W. H. Matchett, Ralph W. Rader, John Traugott, and Robert Weimann. My thanks also to the John Simon Guggenheim Memorial Foundation, the National Endowment for the Humanities, and the University

of California Humanities Research Foundation: they gave
me fellowships to write a different book and allowed this
one to write itself instead. A very different version of part
of Chapter 1 was published in *Shakespeare 1971,* edited
by Clifford Leech and J. M. R. Margeson and published by
the University of Toronto Press in 1972; Chapter 2 is a
revised version of an article that appeared in *Shakespeare
Quarterly* in 1977; and part of Chapter 4 is a revised and
enlarged version of an essay that first appeared in *Four
Essays on Romance,* edited by Herschel Baker, Harvard
University Press, 1971. I gratefully acknowledge permission to include the new versions of this material. John
Hollander's poem, "Hobbes, 1651," is reprinted from
*Spectral Emanations, New and Selected Poems by John Hollan-
der,* copyright © 1962, 1978, by John Hollander, reprinted
by permission of Atheneum Publishers. I am grateful to
Gene Waith for his continued and valued combination of
inspiriting support and uncompromising criticism; though I
cannot hope to have satisfied him on every point, his
rigorous reading improved my manuscript throughout.
And once again I rejoice in acknowledging my boundless
debt to my wife, Marty.

My greatest debt is recorded in the dedication. My book
found its spark in a disagreement with Joe Barber. He
responded with characteristically selfless generosity and insight. Over the years since then I have discovered how
much of what I was going to say he already knew, and I
have profited, as so many have done, from his ability to
believe in me and my work even when I could hardly do so
myself, and to help me grasp the significance of my own
ideas. Conversation with Joe and Cleo always brought a
particular and unique kind of joy, an impulse to give
thanks. Even in dedicating a book to Joe one feels that one
receives more from him than one gives. Of this book he is
the onlie begetter.

1

Meaning and *The Merchant of Venice*

Literary criticism, as even the popular press reports, is in crisis. Only a generation ago the war between an academic establishment committed to historical and philological studies and a guerrilla band of New Critics waving the banner of exegesis seemed to have been resolved by a permanent consensus, and until very recently, at least in the United States, critical energies have been devoted with little self-questioning to perfecting the technology of interpretation. Only yesterday it was widely assumed that the critic's job was to expound the meaning of literary works. Today, under an extraordinarily swift and many-fronted attack, that consensus is in ruins. The reader-response theories argued in various ways by such critics as Stanley Fish and Norman Holland call into question the power of an imaginative work to elicit a uniform response from its audience; Jacques Derrida and his deconstructive allies see language and art as so intractably self-reflexive as to be incapable of analyzable significance; Harold Bloom argues that all reading is misreading, that one reads well only to find oneself in the mirror.[1] For such critics it is hopeless to talk about plays or poems as if they "mean" anything, a mistake to believe as not only the New Critics but the establishment they replaced did that one could speak for a community that looked out on the same world.

The crisis of confidence has belatedly reached Shakespeare criticism in an aggressive analysis by Richard Levin.[2] Levin attacks the self-aggrandizing approaches to literary criticism taken by a variety of writers who have learned that in order to get their articles and books published they must possess the key that everyone else has missed, the secret hidden from all previous critics and scholars. "One of the most striking features of current criticism of the drama of the English Renaissance," he observes, "has been its remarkable proliferation of reinterpretations or 'new readings' which, if they were accepted, would radically alter our traditional views of a great many of these plays—views held, so far as we can tell, by virtually all spectators and readers down to the present time."[3] A "reading," he argues, has a number of characteristics: it is *"an interpretation of a single literary work," "a complete interpretation of the meaning of the work," "an interpretation of the real as distinguished from the apparent meaning of the work," "a justification of the work," "a justification of a thesis about the work"*; it is *"close," "new,"* and *"a tour de force."*[4] The readings Levin attacks "come from the mainstream of academic criticism of English Renaissance drama."[5] They fall into three main groups: thematic ("thematists very frequently disagree on what central theme any given play is about, yet never question the assumption that it must be about a central theme"),[6] ironic (a play means something other than what it seems to mean), and historical (whether an attempt to find King James in *Measure for Measure* or to explain the play by exploring its Zeitgeist or by examining contemporary marriage laws and customs). There are shrewd exposés of some familiar critical gambits: treating deficiencies or flaws of plays as intentional or at least significant virtues (one recalls Fredson Bowers' embarrassing jeer at Delmore Schwartz's critical arabesque on the virtues of "soldier Aristotle," which he didn't recognize as a typo for "solider Aristotle," in "Among School Children"); engaging in "Fluellenism," a method by which one can see the identity shared by any two or more items, and one used by its nominal inventor to prove the similarity between Henry V and Alexander the Great by demonstrating that both Monmouth and Macedon had rivers, and the rivers had salmon in them; claiming as ironic every apparently straightforward moral statement or apparently decent character; recognizing "Christ figures" in every shadow; seeing every play as about the writing of plays.

Much of the book is a chamber of horrors—aisles of readings each proclaiming its unique virtue ("my theme can lick your theme," as Levin puts it); juxtaposed assertions that plays are tracts, arguments, debates, proofs, analyses, statements, commentaries, critiques, meditations, demonstrations, etc.; knee-jerk refusals to take anything, especially the ending of a play, to mean what it says; preposterous claims for implausible interpretations based on shaky historical "proofs." Bad criticism is a scandal that all of us know and frequently lament. Levin has done a service by bringing it out of the closet, and his debunking, like much of the criticism to which I alluded at the outset, deserves attention.

But bad criticism is not the real problem. Consider a few of the names Levin lists, in bland alphabetical sequence, along with others more obviously deserving of the same contemptuous treatment: Peter Alexander, Don Cameron Allen, W. H. Auden, Jonas Barish, Josephine Waters Bennett, Muriel Bradbrook, Cleanth Brooks, John Russell Brown, Jackson Cope, John Danby, Madelaine Doran, Francis Fergusson, Northrop Frye, Harold C. Goddard, G. B. Harrison, R. B. Heilman, G. K. Hunter, Gabriele Bernhard Jackson, R. J. Kaufmann, Frank Kermode, Alvin Kernan, G. Wilson Knight, L. C. Knights, Robert Knoll, Clifford Leech, J. W. Lever, Harry Levin, Barbara K. Lewalski, Laurence Michel, Winifred Nowottny, Eleanor Prosser, A. P. Rossiter, D. A. Traversi, Virgil K. Whitaker, Glynne Wickham, J. Dover Wilson. All of these critics are demonstrated to be guilty of the excessive claims that Levin finds in his worst examples. No single reader would bestow equal praise on all the critics named above, but few readers would fail to find among them some they most admire. And that is the problem I want to address. Not why there is so much bad criticism: there has always been a lot of it, and the institutional rules of the academic game insure its proliferation. Much more importantly: why is much of the best criticism vulnerable to attacks like Levin's, so that the kinds of theoretical rejection of critical study I mentioned at the outset have been able to find so ready an audience? Unlike Fish and Holland, I shall not conclude that the nature of literature and of individual response to it rules out descriptions of literary works that come close to being definitive; unlike Levin, I do not want to replace interpretation with banal suggestions that instead of looking for "readings" critics should accept a play as a "literal representation of particular human actions"[7] or that they need only engage in more dialogue with one another. I am going to insist that literary works mean, and that there are ways in which we can talk about their meanings. But in order to do so I must try to show what in our best criticism has made it so easy to attack.

1

My test case is *The Merchant of Venice.* I have chosen it, first of all, because it is an acknowledged success which has retained its popularity on and off the stage. Second, it has been a center of as much controversy as any of Shakespeare's plays has aroused, and the controversy has led good critics to real and crucial problems. Third, though as I shall indicate there are still those who argue what I take to be idiosyncratic interpretations, in recent years many of the critics have reached a consensus on the play and in so doing have produced invaluable insights. And finally, for all of its virtues much of the best criticism leaves us with the sense that it has somehow failed to come to grips with or has even in some way denied the existence of essential qualities of the play.

The power of *The Merchant of Venice* has moved actors and audiences, critics and readers to interpretations opposed so diametrically that they seem to have been provoked by different plays. Most disagreements have centered on character. On stage Shylock has run a course between Macklin's savage monster and Irving's martyred gentleman;[8] critical descriptions of Shylock range from a "malevolence . . . diabolically inhuman"[9] whom Shakespeare "clearly detested"[10] to a "scapegoat," an instinctively generous man who reminds his tormentors of the wickedness which they possess in greater measure than he.[11] Inevitably Portia has aroused responses similarly at odds, seeming to many the epitome of the romantic heroine, to some virtually a saint, and to others no more than a "callous barrister" with a trump card up her sleeve;[12] Jessica is an ideal portrait of the Christian convert and a "dishonest and disloyal father-hating minx,"[13] Antonio a model of Christian gentleness and an underground Shylock,[14] Bassanio a romanticized lover and a heartless money-grubber. Similarly Portia's use of the law to defeat Shylock has been seen by some as a brilliant and just device, by others as a malicious and unnecessary piece of conniving.[15]

A typical contention flourishes about the scene in which Shylock, provoked to swear vengeance by his daughter's defection and her plundering of his household, learns from Tubal that one of Antonio's ships is lost. To suggest the complexity of our responses to Shylock at this point I need only remind the reader that he justifies his savage commitment to revenge by claiming it as the mechanical and therefore normal human response to injury, and that the claim, thus reflecting an impoverished sensibility, is the climax of his moving appeal to universal brotherhood: "I

am a Jew. Hath not a Jew eyes? . . . "[16] From moment to
moment, even simultaneously, we respond to signals of
Shylock's injured fatherhood, of his role as heavy father,
of his lighthearted mistreatment at the hands of the neg-
ligible Salerio and Solanio, of his motiveless malignity, and
we try hopelessly to reduce to a single attitude our response to his self-defining scorn for Antonio, whose combination of generosity, passivity, sensibility, and spitting
hatred has itself already led us to mixed feelings.

> SHY. I thank God, I thank God. Is it true, is it true?
> TUB. I spoke with some of the sailors that escap'd the
> wrack.
> SHY. I thank thee, good Tubal, good news, good news!
> Ha, ha! [Heard] in Genoa?
> TUB. Your daughter spent in Genoa, as I heard, one
> night fourscore ducats.
> SHY. Thou stick'st a dagger in me. I shall never see my
> gold again. Fourscore ducats at a sitting, fourscore
> ducats!
> TUB. There came divers of Antonio's creditors in my
> company to Venice that swear he cannot choose but
> break.
> SHY. I am very glad of it. I'll plague him, I'll torture him.
> I am glad of it.
> TUB. One of them show'd me a ring that he had of your
> daughter for a monkey.
> SHY. Out upon her! Thou torturest me, Tubal. It was my
> turkis, I had it of Leah when I was a bachelor. I would
> not have given it for a wilderness of monkeys.
> (III.i.102–23)

More clearly evocative of laughter at Shylock's obsessions
and speech mannerism than other parts of the scene, these
lines nevertheless engage us in a kaleidoscopic shift of
emotion and touch us at the end. At this point in Shakespeare's career his ability to create characters with authen-

tic voices and to effect mercurial changes in his audience's emotions leaped beyond what he had been able to do earlier, and he seems to have become interested in shifting sequences of this kind. For in the exactly contemporary *1 Henry IV* the same thing happens repeatedly, most memorably perhaps when Falstaff's comic defense of himself as he plays Prince Hal in the "play extempore" moves through a climactic series of imperatives—"banish Peto, banish Bardolph, banish Poins"—and an outrageous series of epithets—"sweet Jack Falstaff, kind Jack Falstaff, true Jack Falstaff, valiant Jack Falstaff"—to a suddenly no longer funny repetition of the fact of his age with which he began his speech—"old Jack Falstaff"—and to the heartbreakingly repeated "banish not him thy Harry's company, banish not him thy Harry's company" and the climax, "banish plump Jack, and banish all the world," culminating both the imperative and the comic epithet, and followed by Hal's response, mysteriously appropriate from both the player and the role he plays as Henry IV, "I do, I will" (II.iv.466–81). No one, I believe, misses the emotional complexity of that moment. But at the corresponding moment in *The Merchant of Venice* critic after critic, rather than acknowledging the welter of our responses, insists that this scene reveals a clear and simple truth about Shylock's martyred humanity or his comic villainy.[17]

Such radical disagreements between obviously simplistic critics testify to a fact about their subject that ought to be the point of departure for criticism. Instead, critics both bad and good have constructed strategies to evade the problem posed by divergent responses. Some blame Shakespeare, suggesting that his confusion accounts for tension in the work and its audience.[18] Others appeal to a narrow concept of cultural history which writes off our responses as anachronistic, unavailable to Shakespeare's contemporaries because of their attitudes toward usury or

Jews or comedy.[19] Still others suggest that, since the plays are fragile confections designed to display engaging if implausible characters, exegetical criticism is misplaced.[20] Though all of these strategies attract modern practitioners, they have lost ground before the dominant evasion, the reduction of the play to a theme which, when we understand it, tells us which of our responses we must suppress. The ingenious thematic critic, so adroitly delineated by Richard Levin, is licensed to stipulate that "in terms of the structure of the play Shylock is a minor character" and can be ignored,[21] or that the action is only metaphorical and does not need to be examined as if its events literally happened,[22] or that Shylock is only a Jew, or a banker, or a usurer, or a man spiritually dead, or a commentary on London life, never a combination of these;[23] or that *The Merchant of Venice* is built on "four levels of existence" corresponding to Dante's divisions—"Hell (Shylock), Purgatory proper (Antonio) and the Garden of Eden (Portia-Bassanio), and Paradise";[24] or that the play is exclusively about love, or whatever, and, insofar as it doesn't fit the critic's formulation, it is flawed.[25]

2

My chief concern here, as I said above, is not with such dismal stuff but rather with a less obviously procrustean kind of criticism which, accepting the play as a whole, attempts to account for its unity without expelling characters or issues or plot. The new consensus is laconically summarized by Frank Kermode:

> *The Merchant of Venice* is "about" judgment, redemption and mercy; the supersession in human history of the grim four thousand years of unalleviated justice by the era of love and mercy. It begins with usury and corrupt love; it ends with harmony and perfect love. And all the time it tells its audience that this is its

subject; only by a determined effort to avoid the obvious can one mistake the theme of *The Merchant of
Venice*.[26]

In this view, developed by John Russell Brown, C. L.
Barber, John Palmer, Lawrence Danson, and others,[27] the
wealth so mechanistically prized by Shylock is set against
what Brown calls "love's wealth," possessiveness against
prodigality, giving against taking. For Barber, "the whole
play dramatizes the conflict between the mechanisms of
wealth and the masterful, social use of it."[28] Problems that
stumped other critics have been resolved. The bond plot is
related to the casket plot, for example, by the positing of a
central theme. In Brown's words:

> Shall we say it is a play about give and take?—about
> conundrums such as the more you give, the more you
> get, or, to him that hath shall be given, and from him
> that hath not, shall be taken away even that which he
> hath? The two parts of the play are linked by these
> problems: Portia is the golden fleece, the merchants
> venture and hazard as any lover; the caskets deal all in
> value, the bond and the rings are pledges of posses-
> sion.[29]

One of the most comprehensive accounts to date is John
R. Cooper's "Shylock's Humanity," which argues that at
the play's core is a theological distinction between the
values of Christianity and those of a Pauline version of Old
Testament Judaism.[30] This view, essentially shared by the
group of critics I have been discussing, and carried to an
extreme by the man who sees the play as a Shakespearean
Commedia, sets the law, a rational principle according to
which men should get exactly what they deserve, against
Christian mercy, which gives freely to those who hazard all
they possess. Cooper notes that not all the Christians in
the play act like ideal Christians—a fact on which a number

of schematic interpretations founder—and argues that

> the fundamental opposition in the play is not between
> Jew and Christian but between two sets of values. On
> the one hand, there is the uncalculating generosity
> and forgiveness, the sense of one's own unworthiness
> and the infinite value of others, the attitude referred
> to by Portia as "mercy." On the other hand, there is
> the hard-headed attitude of those who have a high
> estimation of their own value and rights, and who
> demand just payment for themselves, whether in the
> form of money, or revenge, or a wife.[31]

In this account as in others the opposition in the play is
seen as symbolized by the inscriptions on the caskets:
Morocco trusts appearances and puts his faith in gold as
Shylock does; Arragon demands what he deserves, insisting
like Shylock on a rational justice; both are beaten by Bassanio, who gives and hazards all. The opposition is seen
by some as figured in the symbolic connotations of the
metals of which the caskets are made, and by most as embodied geographically in Belmont, home of music and love,
and the commercial Venice.

If I suggest that these critics are wrong, I shall have
gravely misstated my argument. What they describe is
there, and reflecting on our experience of the play we
recognize the patterns identified. Their analysis integrates
the techniques developed in the last half-century for literary study and, perhaps more important, arises from unmistakably personal experiences of the play. Thus they
hear verbal nuances and know how to talk about them;
they know the significance of motifs and echoes, of
dramaturgic and metrical effect, of structure and symbol,
character and genre. Yet even their own writing conveys a
sense of uneasy tentativeness that speaks of more than
simple modesty or rhetorical disclaimer. In the first passage I cited, for example, Kermode puts eloquent quota-
tion marks around the word "about" when he tells us what

the play is "about." Palmer, less insistent than some critics that the theme really dominates the play, seems dubious even about as much theme as he asserts: "Nothing is further from Shakespeare's mind than to convey a lesson. But the lesson is there, product of a perfectly balanced and sensitive mind intent upon the dramatic presentation of human realities."[32] I quoted before Barber's capsule summary of the theme: "The whole play dramatizes the conflict between the mechanism of wealth and the masterful, social use of it." But listen to the reservations implied by the sentence that follows: "The happy ending, which abstractly considered as an event is hard to credit, and the treatment of Shylock, which abstractly considered as justice is hard to justify, work as we actually watch or read the play because these events express relief and triumph in the achievement of a distinction." And later, after his demonstration of the total efficiency with which the play communicates its complex set of interrelated judgments on character, wealth, and love so that the audience is clearly instructed by the end: "I must add, after all this praise for the way the play makes its distinctions about the use of wealth, that *on reflection,* not when viewing or reading the play, but when thinking about it, I find the distinction, as others have, somewhat too easy."[33] And he goes on, with characteristic sensitivity, to demonstrate how much of the play—Portia's facile generosity, Shylock's comeuppance, Antonio's fudging of the usury argument, Shylock's large place in our consciousness—fails to fit even so subtle a schematization as he had made. Brown, you will recall, presents his summary as a question: "Shall we say it is a play about . . . ?" and I suggest that his rhetorical choice reflects a tacit acknowledgment that in some sense the formulation is narrower than the play. Look at the sentences immediately preceding his question: "So *The Merchant of Venice* dances to its conclusion, its many elements mingling together joyfully. Perhaps when the dance is in progress, it is undesirable to look too closely for a pattern.

But the dance does satisfy, and it is worth while trying to find out why."[34] Or, in a passage from another essay on the play: "Because such judgments are not made explicit in the play, we, as an audience in the theatre, may never become consciously aware of them; we would almost certainly fail in our response if, during performance, our whole attention was given to recognizing and elucidating such judgments."[35]

Why, if as I have claimed the criticism of these men adds up to a synthesis that comes closer than anything before it to explaining the play, is their presentation so hedged? I suggest that they recognize that they have not in fact explained the very things that provoked them to the elucidation of meaning in the first place, the questions that the play like any good play raises in order to drive us to search for answers that are not forthcoming. Each critic in his own way suggests some conflict between the thematic pattern he identifies on reflection and his actual experience of the play. Barber, whose major contribution in *Shakespeare's Festive Comedy* consists, after all, in far more original, useful, and exhilarating modes of criticism than the thematic formulation I have excerpted here, addresses the problem himself:

> No figure in the carpet is the carpet. There is in the pointing out of patterns something that is opposed to life and art, an ungraciousness which artists in particular feel and resent. Readers feel it too, even critics: for every new moment, every new line or touch, is a triumph of opportunism, something snatched in from life beyond expectation and made design beyond design. And yet the fact remains that it is as we see the design that we see design undone and brought alive.[36]

If on reflection, through the contemplation of thematic patterns, we manage to be satisfied by an understanding that seems to resolve the constant inner conflict which the process of *The Merchant of Venice* sets going in us, we do so by treating as accidental rather than substantive the doubts with which we are left by the end.

Consider some of the problems that remain unresolved in the versions of the comedy we have been discussing. Present in only five scenes, Shylock speaks fewer than four hundred lines yet dominates the play, haunting our memories during the suddenly etherealized and equally suddenly trivialized final episodes as we try to reach a simple position on the fairness of his treatment, or even on the truth of his response to it, funny, deflated, proud, inscrutable: "I pray you give me leave to go from hence, / I am not well" (IV.i.395–96). The play, we are told, is about the opposition of mercy to legalism. Cooper, subtle enough to realize that the distinction must not be made by separating out Christian lambs and Jewish goats, must nonetheless belie our own experience of the play, as he admits, in order to judge the disposition of the villain: "Though his forced conversion to Christianity seems to us to be cruel and insulting, we are meant, I think and as many critics have said, to see this as the altogether kindly conversion of Shylock to the new rule of mercy and thus his liberation from the dilemma of the old Law."[37] Note how that "we are meant," derived not from Cooper's response to something he sees as "cruel and insulting" but from a thesis about what the play means, denies to Shakespeare's intention or the play's virtue what the comedy actually *does* to us. Abstractly considered, Shylock's enforced conversion might be judged benevolent, in that it is imposed upon him in order to assure his salvation. Not only is that salvation not mentioned, however, but the conversion is dictated as part of a settlement that is otherwise entirely fiscal, without any suggestion of kindness:

> So please my lord the Duke and all the court
> To quit the fine for one half of his goods,
> I am content; so he will let me have

> The other half in use, to render it
> Upon his death to the gentleman
> That lately stole his daughter.
> Two things provided more, that for this favor
> He presently become a Christian;
> The other, that he do record a gift,
> Here in the court, of all he dies possess'd
> Unto his son Lorenzo and his daughter. (IV.i.380–90)

If Antonio's plea for the mitigation of Shylock's sentence is a step back from the cruelty of the Duke's original plan, it nevertheless insists twice that all of the Jew's property must eventually fall into the hands of "the gentleman / That lately stole his daughter"; and one doubts whether any actress could make Portia's demand that Shylock not only accept the judgment but profess satisfaction with it—"Art thou contented, Jew? what dost thou say?"— sound "altogether kindly." The issue is not how Elizabethans felt about the relative advantages of dying in or outside the church, but how Shakespeare forces his audience to respond to this particular conversion in its context.

For Barber our response to Shylock is a problem, but, like some critics whose work his supplants, he suggests that in that respect the play failed because Shakespeare cared more about his villain than his purpose could afford. But Cooper has the superior technology, and his conclusion is cleaner: we must deny that we even care about Shylock's harsh dismissal and his forced conversion so that we may feel, in Brown's phrase, all the elements of the play "mingling together joyfully." How much more considerate both of art and of our response to it is Stanley Cavell's observation in an essay entitled "A Matter of Meaning It":

> The artist is responsible for everything that happens in his work—and not just in the sense that it is done, but in the sense that it is *meant*. It is a terrible re-

sponsibility; very few men have the gift and the pa-
tience to shoulder it. But it is all the more terrible,
when it *is* shouldered, not to appreciate it, to refuse to
understand something meant so well.[38]

3

> In Belmont is a lady richly left,
> And she is fair and, fairer than that word,
> Of wondrous virtues. Sometimes from her eyes
> I did receive fair speechless messages.
> Her name is Portia, nothing undervalu'd
> To Cato's daughter, Brutus' Portia.
> Nor is the wide world ignorant of her worth,
> For the four winds blow in from every coast
> Renowned suitors, and her sunny locks
> Hang on her temples like a golden fleece,
> Which makes her seat of Belmont Colchis' strond,
> And many Jasons come in quest of her.
> O my Antonio, had I but the means
> To hold a rival place with one of them,
> I have a mind presages me such thrift
> That I should questionless be fortunate! (I.i.161–76)

If Quiller-Couch and, alas, too many modern directors can
dismiss Bassanio as a mere fortune hunter, we have been
instructed to a more complex judgment: though he is indeed interested in Portia's money, Bassanio does not, as
Shylock does, let money take the place of values that matter more, and so as a social Christian he is allowed to have
it. Shylock loves only gold, material substance, we are told,
while Bassanio loves Portia as well as gold; after all, he
compares her with Brutus's Portia. Yet Bassanio's way of
comparing his Portia to Brutus's is to say that the one is
"nothing undervalu'd" to the other; he praises her first for
being rich and then for being fair; it is the ambiguous
quality of "worth" that draws the world to her; his game is
thrift and his hope is to be fortunate; and he sees himself as

Jason stealing the golden fleece—a legend later reduced to its crassest implications by Gratiano (III.ii.239–41). And of course Morocco's crazy apostrophe to the gold casket (II.vii.36–60) will reveal exactly the same confusion of values as Bassanio's speech, echoing its images and language and even its word "undervalu'd" (l. 53)—and only moments before we hear of Shylock's similar confusion between his daughter and his ducats. How is Morocco really guilty when Bassanio is not? Portia's true gold may be spiritual, but Bassanio gets himself out of trouble with his creditors by her material wealth. Furthermore, if we are to believe that his superiority consists in his ability to tell reality from appearance, we are not allowed to forget that Portia of the beautiful soul is also a beautiful woman, a romantic as well as a commercial prize. She herself is delighted to be rid of Morocco because of his looks: "Let all of his complexion choose me so," she says as he leaves, and insofar as the word points to temper as it does to appearance, inner as well as outer, it suggests a correspondence between looks and character that the casket plot seems to be denying.

The thematic values identified by those who see the play as a conflict between the Hebrew and Christian dispensations point to rejection of the wealth returned in abundance to the Christian company and to a demonstration of the virtue of impoverished love. That the comic resolution demands worldly success as well, a return of more than has in fact been hazarded, suggests a conflict between Christianity and comedy as deep as the one generally seen between it and tragedy.[39] If, as Brown says, the comic point is that those already rich spiritually are materially enriched by the happy outcome, my point is that constant signals in the play imply that it isn't all so simple and that they keep us from the single-minded joy Brown sees as our final state. Everything Brown says is there, and yet by the end we are not so sure that it resolves the tensions the play has aroused in us.

One might discuss at length other elements in the play that cause uneasiness in an audience and difficulties for a critic who wants to make a schematic analysis—the pointed contrast between a Belmont and a Venice not really so different from one another; the peculiar characterization of the melancholy Antonio, the link between his sadness and Portia's in their opening lines, and the fact that the play is named after him; the ring plot which, though it enables Portia to teach once again her lesson about bonds and love, reminds us of her trickery and her tendency to domineer, so inconsistent with the moving spontaneity of her emotions both as Bassanio chooses the lead casket and as she speaks of mercy. But I shall cite, and briefly, only two matters.

First, the characterization of Lorenzo and Jessica has been disputed often enough to suggest that their ambivalence is built into the play. The judgments of their best critics reflect difficulty with them. Goddard sees their villainy as necessary to prod Shylock to revenge. Burckhardt condemns them as an inversion of the true bonded love of the play's theme, lawless and mean-spirited, "spendthrift rather than liberal, thoughtless squanderers of stolen substance," trading for a monkey "the ring which ought to seal their love."[40] Yet Brown sees them as exemplars of "the central theme of love's wealth." He too sees them as squanderers, but in "joyful celebration"; he praises their *"unthrift* love" and argues that if Jessica's "reckless prodigality is a fault, it is a generous one and an understandable excess after the restriction of her father's precept."[41] Plainly Lorenzo and Jessica subvert any schematic reading of the play. If, for example, some signals suggest that the conversion forced on Shylock is an act of kindness, Lorenzo makes us resist that interpretation of Christian treatment of the Jew:

> she hath directed
> How I shall take her from her father's house,

> What gold and jewels she is furnish'd with,
> What page's suit she hath in readiness.
> If e'er the Jew her father come to heaven,
> It will be for his gentle daughter's sake,
> And never dare misfortune cross her foot,
> Unless she do it under this excuse,
> That she is issue to a faithless Jew. (II.iv.29–37)

If, as Burckhardt thinks, Lorenzo and Jessica help silhouette Portia's genuine value, their presence in Belmont and their common cause with her against Shylock complicate the play for interpretation, as does the strange excursus on music that Lorenzo delivers in the last act.

And that takes me to my second matter, the beads of language, imagery, and ideas threaded on the string of music. It is a commonplace that that music—the music of the heavenly choirs, the music that Portia has sounded as Bassanio makes his choice—accompanies the life of grace, sensibility, love, and play, the life won by those who triumph in the play, while Shylock hates "the vile squealing of the wry-neck'd fife" (II.v.29ff.) and mocks those who "cannot contain their urine" "when the bagpipe sings i' th' nose" (IV.1.49–50). As Lorenzo puts it, the play seems to say:

> The man that hath no music in himself,
> Nor is not moved with concord of sweet sounds,
> Is fit for treasons, stratagems, and spoils;
>
> .   .   .   .   .   .
>
> Let no such man be trusted.
>
> (V.i.83–88)

But Lorenzo is a poor witness, since "treasons, stratagems, and spoils" characterizes his exploits at least as accurately as it does those of Shylock, who has other personality problems. Furthermore, Lorenzo's dialogue with Jessica is sandwiched between the episodes of Portia's stratagem against Bassanio, the ring plot, and helps both to undercut the enormous emotional claim she has made on the audience in the trial scene and to call attention to the triviality at best of the game she plays with the ring. We might note also that the chief other entry of music into the play is the song that Portia has sung during Bassanio's ordeal with the caskets, and interestingly that song has occasioned a still unsettled debate as to whether it is simply a pretext to suggest "lead" through rhymes with "bred," "head," and the like.

4

Once again, my point is not that critics who are demonstrably right about so much are to be dismissed, lightly or otherwise. But one may justifiably ask how so much brain power in the most sensitive and highly trained critical audiences has produced so little that can't be punctured simply by watching one's own responses to details of a play. One may ask furthermore why critical readings of similar methodology and equal brilliance by critics of different temperaments so often add up to radically opposed interpretations. My guess is that our troubles stem in good part from the value we have put on reductiveness. We have been betrayed by a bias toward what can be set out in rational argument. Before the full impact of the new romantic understanding of art hit the professional study of literature, that bias reflected itself in the decision of literary scholars to concentrate on matters now seen as less than central to the understanding of the work itself. But, under the delayed influence of Coleridge and his contemporaries in England and Germany, literary study began to realize how far it was from dealing with the experience of art and began to come closer to it by focusing on the interpretation of texts. To be responsible, however, the newer study had to produce conclusions which were derived as logically and argued as closely as demonstrations of source and influence had been. Attracted by the spectacular possibilities of a new technology—Empson of course wanted to irritate with his arbitrary precision, but was nonetheless pleased to be able to number the types of ambiguity—critics fell into an invisible trap, the fallacy of misplaced concreteness: what can be brought by self-contained argument to a satisfying conclusion is what is worth discussing, and responses that don't work into the argument must be discounted. Given a romantic inheritance, given a genuine sense of the integrity of a single poem or play or novel, given a puritanical bias which assumes that the value of literature is moral and familiarly expresses itself in the notion of the professor of literature as lay preacher, given a long history of assumption that art is valuable at least half because of what it teaches, and given an art which is verbal, so that virtually all the patterns, parallels, structural juxtapositions, image clusters, ironic repetitions, variations, and generic conventions a critic can find can be translated into other words, was it not inevitable that the bias toward a criticism that would produce discrete and rational arguments should culminate in the study of meaning?

There is nothing surprising about our bias towards rationality. It is perfectly consistent with our hopes for civilization, with our needs, both inner- and outer-directed, to write prose that is logical, coherent, defensible, documentable. And the critical paradigm that establishes meaning as the principle of unity in a work and our experience of it is consistent with patterns that *do* exist in the plays—otherwise I could not have distinguished among the kinds of criticisms I have discussed—and that need to be explicated. But it is time to recall that all intellection is reductive, and that the closer an intellectual system comes to full internal consistency and universality of application—as with Newtonian mechanics—the more obvious become the exclusiveness of its preoccupations and the limitations of its value. What our successful criticism of meaning has made clear—and I include not only naive

Meaning and *The Merchant of Venice*

reduction but also that much more sophisticated criticism which argued so cogently against the heresy of paraphrase while still being concerned with summary thematic statements[42]—is its consistent suppression of the nature of aesthetic experience.

Should it not have disturbed critics interested in hypostatizing meaning that no two critics of any play really agree with one another in their formulations, that no two performances reflect identical interpretations or produce uniform responses in their audiences, that all of us return to plays we know intimately to discover that we respond to them in entirely new ways? Is not the disagreement about works of art as significant a fact for the critic as the interpretation he favors? Might a fruitful criticism not begin and end there as validly as it does with reduction to thematic descriptions of unity?

Confidence in our methodology has enabled us over the years to sidestep the implications of what we know about the creative act. No reputable critic would attempt to validate his analysis by claiming that the meaning he extracts was in the author's conscious and explicit intention, and even poets now accept the thesis that what the critic reveals in their work, no matter how unfamiliar to them, may have been a dominant factor in preconscious activity during composition. Even E. D. Hirsch, the literary theorist who states most insistently that meaning is entirely a product of authorial control—a position with which, as will shortly become clear, I do not myself disagree—readily grants that "it is very possible to mean what one is not conscious of meaning."[43] Now if we validly appeal to pre- or subconscious layers of the artist's experience, we ought to be ready to do the same for the audience, whose experience of a theme may be just as remote from consciousness. And if we do so wholeheartedly, we are likely to find little reason why an abstract idea should have been the central factor either in creation or in audience experience, particularly when that idea must inevitably be stated as a "meaning" on which no two experiences of the work can agree.

"One thematist's gestalt is not another's," Richard Levin justly observes, and he shrewdly demonstrates how critics attempting to make more inclusive and definitive thematic statements than their predecessors remain trapped in hermeneutic solipsism (a point similar to one made earlier by E. D. Hirsch).[44] Acknowledging that even "good" critics do the same thing as "bad" ones, admitting that he cannot find any model to replace the pernicious critical mode he attacks, Levin nevertheless fails to recognize the dimensions of the problem he is dealing with. And, directing his scrutiny exclusively to the performance of critics, he fails equally to recognize the ultimate cause of our critical sins: the experience of literature. A play we care about provokes us to form a gestalt, and the powerful experience of doing so may tempt us to formulate it thematically. Our formulations differ widely enough to enable Levin's mockery, and they are inadequate enough to serve very poorly, as I have tried to show, what is communicated by the plays they describe. Nevertheless, even at their worst they speak for the conflicts, tensions, implications, and significant fields of force that contribute to our sense that a play is an autonomous, coherent, and meaningful whole. To repudiate that sense because critics have too often translated it into excessively narrow thematic formulations, as Levin does, or to argue that it is too subjective to allow for descriptions of the common experience of an audience, as Norman Holland does,[45] is to deny the possibility of authorial communication or communal aesthetic experience, to deny that at a certain level of experience a work of art controls the responses of audiences who share its culture, even though each member of the audience may interpret those responses differently.[46] The eddying signals communicated by a play arouse a total and complex involvement of our intellect, our moral sensibility, our need to complete incomplete patterns and answer questions, our longing to judge, and that involvement is so incessantly in motion that to pin it down to a "meaning" is to negate its very essence.

The essence of our experience is our haunting sense of what doesn't fit the thesis we are tempted at every moment to derive. If one hallmark of an authentic work of art and a central source of its power is its ability to drive us to search out its central mystery, another way may be its ultimate irreducibility to a schema. Both of these qualities are present in Shakespeare's plays. They are there because Shakespeare put them there. If we are going to call the distillation of our experience of one of the plays its meaning, we must acknowledge that it includes both the paradigm to which the controlling patterns of the play tempt us to reduce our experience and elements of that experience which resist or weaken or complicate or contradict the paradigm. It is this whole, "meant so well," to which Stanley Cavell points when he claims that "the artist is responsible for everything that happens in his work—and not just in the sense that it is done, but in the sense that it is *meant.*" Both the evidence of the critical consensus and the evidence of rational disagreement in the interpretation of a play like *The Merchant of Venice* lead us back to a particularly powerful authorial control all too susceptible of simplistic hypostatization. It is the critic's job, considering the evidence of others' responses as well as his own, to comprehend as much as possible of what is contained in the intention of a work. "All valid interpretation of every sort," as E. D. Hirsch puts it, "is founded on the re-cognition of what an author meant.[47]

Like many insights that have attained widespread acceptance, Keat's definition of "negative capability" has been allowed to lose its cutting edge.[48] If Keats speaks as rightly as I think he does for artists and for us as their audiences, then the critic must learn to defer his "irritable reaching after fact and reason" and learn to think of "uncertainties, mysteries, doubts" as the stuff of our experience of art. To put it another way, he must treat experience as the subject of discussions of art. That is the point of John Dewey's profound and too little heeded *Art as Experience,* which sees the creation of art and the response to it as quintessentially like life, characterized by process, tension, resistance, and an ineffable sense of integrity. Keats's insight is implicit in the criticism of Kenneth Burke, who has insisted on asking what the poem does for the poet and his readers rather than what it says, who sees a play by Shakespeare as "a device for the arousing and fulfilling of expectations in an audience," and who has defined "the symbolic act" as *"the dancing of an attitude."*[49] For Dewey and Burke the job of the critic is to analyze in the work a set of highly complex interrelations among its elements which the audience, experiencing those elements as they are presented, perceives as a unity. And for Dewey and Burke form and content are inseparable because the experience of the work is one—hence "the dancing of an attitude."

That phrase, strikingly similar to Brown's reading of *The Merchant of Venice* as a dance, tempts one to wonder how much of Burke's power derives from his having first been a music critic. René Wellek, developing a theory of literature, could, despite all his better intentions, validate the seach for meaning by calling the work of art "a system of norms of ideal *concepts* which are intersubjective."[50] But the music critic cannot look for a conceptual content at the center of a work's intention and power. The attraction of the word "theme" for literary critics may be its musical implications, but its prime meaning as they use it is its older lexical meaning, the text of a sermon or the subject of a discourse. For the musicologist a theme is generally one among several, and it is never to be confused with meaning. If he wants to discuss meaning, the music critic has no choice but to study in minute particularity the ways in which at each point a composition arouses and fulfills, or fails to fulfill, an audience's expectations. A new criticism of Shakespeare might well begin with the music analysis of Leonard B. Meyer. Morally concerned with music as an art that communicates, Meyer has derived from gestalt theory instruments for the analysis of the artwork's complex and significant control of its audience's responses. Interestingly, he is concerned with devices very much like those that have attracted literary critics of recent generations: the use of one phrase to make us think of another, recurrence, variation, parallelism, the apparent emergence of pattern out of linked details. But he is not interested in the kind of reduction that such discovery generally elicits from literary critics.[51]

The good Shakespeare critic must point out the patterns of the dance. He must find terms in which the oppositions and conflicts and problems within a play can be stated while recognizing the reductiveness of those terms. He must fight the temptation to proclaim what it boils down to; he must fight against the urge to closure which, as a gifted audience, he feels with particular intensity. He must learn to point to the centers of energy and turbulence in a play without regarding them as coded elements of a thematic formula. And while rejecting narrow conclusions drawn by other critics, he must be able to learn from the perceptions that have led to those conclusions.

One need only describe such a hypothetical paragon to recognize that such critics already exist. Two of those to whose thematic statements I have objected, C. L. Barber and John Russell Brown, more characteristically employ enormously suggestive and nonreductionist methodologies; the latter has himself argued repeatedly for a theatrical recreation of Shakespeare that will not try to pin the plays down to interpretations that constrict the range of meanings in them. Other exemplars come readily to mind.

Meaning and *The Merchant of Venice*

Maynard Mack's already classic essay on "The Jacobean Shakespeare" treats patterns with the imagination and respect generally accorded only to meanings (as if most critics were driven by their irritable reaching after fact and reason always to shout, like Amy Lowell, "Christ, what are patterns for?") Stephen Booth's goal is to contribute to "an analytic criticism that does not sacrifice—or at least tries not to sacrifice—any of a work of literature to logical convenience or even to common sense," and he infuriatingly refuses to find a conclusion in the turbulence he demonstrates in Shakespeare. Marvin Rosenberg's historical criticism, based on the history of performance, demands that we build into our understanding of the greatest tragedies the full range of interpretations they have provoked. Susan Snyder demonstrates "that tragedy's ground is the disputed border—or no-man's-land—between a just and orderly pattern for life on the one hand and an amoral patternlessness on the other," and studies the complexity produced by generic signals rather than thematic simplicity. E. A. J. Honigmann has made a strong case that we value Shakespeare as we do "partly because forcing secret and contrary impressions upon us, [he] makes us work harder," and that though we share our experience with the rest of the spectators on a given occasion, our "various responses mix," "interpenetrate one another and may not be tidily unscrambled." Michael Goldman has demonstrated how far-reaching, subtle, and lucid a criticism may be when it is based on attending to how the plays make our bodies feel. And an extraordinary group of new psychoanalytic critics, including Janet Adelman, C. L. Barber, Coppélia Kahn, Arthur C. Kirsch, Murry M. Schwartz, Meredith Skura, Richard Wheeler, and others—have succeeded brilliantly by rejecting the formulas and reductive tropes of the psychoanalytic criticism of earlier generations.[52] No one reading the great number of new books on Shakespeare being published every year can fail to notice—*pace* Levin—that surprisingly many of them are valuable and

permanent contributions to our knowledge and understanding; no one attending annual meetings of the Shakespeare Association of America, or other gatherings where
new ideas about Shakespeare are discussed, can fail to
come away at least as excited by the sense that we are
making communal progress in our understanding of
Shakespeare and of the nature of art as he is dismayed by
the prevalence of naive and self-aggrandizing critical
reductiveness.

5

The challenge to criticism, I have been suggesting, is to
embark on a self-conscious reconsideration of the
phenomena that our technology has enabled us to explore,
to consider the play as a dynamic interaction between artist
and audience, to learn to talk about the process of our
involvement rather than our considered view after the
aesthetic event. We need to find concepts other than
meaning to account for the end of a play, the sense of
unverbalizable coherence, lucidity, and unity that makes
us know we have been through a single, significant, and
shared experience. We need to learn to distinguish between the art represented in its extreme form by the murder mystery, in which the end completes the gestalt figure
that tells us unequivocally how we should have responded
to every detail along the way, and Shakespeare's profounder art, an art no less powerful in drawing us to a final
vantage point from which we may look back over the
whole, but an art ultimately irreducible to an explanatory
schema.

To get down to cases, what can we do with *The Merchant
of Venice?* Two obvious places to begin are its genre and its
history, both on stage and in the study, and in both places
we come immediately to the same realization. *The Merchant of Venice* is a comedy, inviting us to celebrate a happy
resolution and the reassertion of the values of a commu-

nity that includes us. Shakespeare's comedy normally involves the overthrow of a threat, often the ejection of a character whose inability to participate in the communal resolution threatens community itself. But *The Merchant of Venice* plays on that convention by investing enough of our emotions in its outsider to make us at least uneasy about his discomfiture; the play unsettles one's normal reaction to the end of a comedy. So much is indicated by the centuries of reaction to Shylock and concomitantly to other characters that I indicated earlier. I hope I have made it clear that audience responses to Shylock or Bassanio or Portia which are alternately or exclusively hostile or sympathetic are the result of ambivalent signals built into the play. The countless such signals in *The Merchant of Venice* are part of an entire system. If for a moment, or an entire production, we are led to respond sympathetically to Shylock, we necessarily respond with less sympathy to Jessica or Portia, and vice versa. The potential fullness of a reading in which one element or another in the play can come to seem like the center of the play's values and the focus of its allegiances is paradoxically the source of both its inexhaustible complexity and its vulnerability to powerful productions in which the play seems to belong completely to Shylock or to Belmont. The best reading and the best production, one might guess, would have to take account of the possibilities of both readings.

As the critical consensus has repeatedly shown in recent years, the terms in which the central conflicts of *The Merchant of Venice* can be paraphrased or summarized are remarkably clear. As the entire critical history of the play has made equally apparent, the play's ultimate resolution of those conflicts is anything but clear or simple. The deep polarities in the comedy are luminously evident long before the end. The life-and-death struggle between them makes us feel the need to take a stand on one side or the other. And yet the same play that makes that demand refuses to permit an unequivocal resolution in favor of one

character or group of characters or one term in a thematic
debate. The way in which an unresolvably problematic
sense of human experience is built into the structure of the
play can be suggested by an attempt to list some of the
incompatible elements, provocative of inconsistent responses, that must be included in an adequate description
of each of the polarities the play develops. On the one side,
as we have seen, we find Shylock, trickery, anality, precise
definition, possessiveness, contempt for prodigality, legalism, the Old Testament, Jews, dislocated values,
mechanistic ethics and psychology, a fondness for bonds,
stinginess, a wronged father, a conventional comic butt, an
outsider, a paradoxical honesty about intention, a repressive father, distrust of emotion and hatred of music, bad
luck, and failure. On the other we find Portia, but also
Antonio, Bassanio, Lorenzo, Jessica, and Gratiano; free-
dom, metaphorical richness in language, prodigality, tran-
scendence of the law, intense commitment to legalism,
stealing, the New Testament, Christians; values that sometimes seem simple and right, sometimes complex and
right, sometimes complex and wrong; love, generosity,
cruelty to a father, life within a charmed circle, self-
deception about motivation, youth rebelling against conventional comic repressive fatherhood, love of emotion
and music, supreme trickery, a fondness for bonds, good
luck, success.

At every point at which we want simplicity we get complexity. Some signals point to coherence—thus the conflict
between the ideas of prodigality and possessiveness, or
between two definitions of prodigality. But just as many
create discomfort, point to centrifugality—virtually every
mention of a ring and every episode involving one, the
grouping of characters, the links between scenes that
constantly ask us to reassess what we've just seen and interpreted in terms of what we're now seeing. In terms of
moral content that we can extract, we come away with
precious little: by the end we know as we knew before we

began that cruelty is bad and love better, just as we know in *King Lear* that love between fathers and daughters is a good thing. If *The Merchant of Venice* or any of Shakespeare's great plays were to be judged by what we can claim to have learned from it, or by its ability to lead critics to clear formulations that agree with each other, society would pay even less for English departments than it does now. Yet by the end we have been through a constantly turbulent experience which demands an incessant giving and taking back of allegiance, a counterpoint of ever-shifting response to phrase, speech, character, scene, action, a welter of emotions and ideas and perceptions and surprises and intuitions of underlying unity and coherence rivalled only by our experience in the real world so perplexingly suggested by the artifact to which we yield ourselves.

I have called this chapter "Meaning and *The Merchant of Venice*." I have voiced reservations about readings of *The Merchant of Venice* that have claimed to be able to make precise formulations of its meaning, and have tried to show that such attempts are inadequate to the experience of the play. At the same time I have argued against critical positions that, recognizing the shortcomings of such attempts to stipulate meaning, would assert that a play has no meaning, and I have suggested that, despite other inadequate paraphrases, *The Merchant of Venice* does have a meaning. The time would seem to have arrived for me to attempt my own statement of that meaning. I hope that it is clear by now, however, that I do not think that the meaning that is there can be stated as a thematic paradigm. The power of the play is its power to create the illusion of a life that is like our lives, a world like our world, in which as in our life and our world experience tempts us to believe itself to be reducible to fundamental terms but cannot be adequately analyzed in those terms. In *The Merchant of Venice* as in the life we live outside the theater we are driven to formulate questions which—despite the fact that we manage to go on living our lives—we cannot begin to answer. The problem is the one with which Kant begins the *Critique of Pure Reason:*

> Human reason has this peculiar fate that in one species of its knowledge it is burdened by questions which, as prescribed by the very nature of reason itself, it is not able to ignore, but which, as transcending all its powers, it is also not able to answer.[53]

We can neither ignore nor answer the questions with which our reason is burdened. It is this quality of our existence that is ultimately suggested by our being tempted to and frustrated by the search for meaning in *The Merchant of Venice,* this conviction that the world makes sense but that the sense once abstracted no longer fits it. The attempt to state the meaning of the play is therefore not much more likely to produce an accurate account than an attempt to state the meaning of life. But to say that we cannot profitably talk about the meaning of life is not to say that life is meaningless. *The Merchant of Venice* is a model of our experience, showing us that we need to live as if life has meaning and rules, yet insisting that the meaning is ultimately ineffable and the rules are provisional. The experience of the play, like the experience of a sonata—or of life itself—is one of process, and involves not just a final cadence or even the recapitulation of some main themes, but a whole sequence of contrasting but related developments. That is why Dewey's consideration of art as experience and of experience as process remains so important. Properly understood, the play as a whole is identical with its meaning.

To argue thus is perhaps to declare one's continuity with the New Critical tradition, as it has recently been described with brilliance and something less than admiration by Gerald Graff: to endow "texts with the most complicated of meanings" while seeming "to call into question the notion that a literary work could even possess anything

so didactic as a meaning,"[54] " 'denying,' " in words Graff
quotes from Hazard Adams, " 'the adequacy of any critical
statement and constantly urging us to look again.' "[55]
Though I do not share the tendency sometimes ascribed to
the New Critics to see literature as nonreferential, as having no connection with a world outside, I obviously do
share their paradoxical interest in scrutinizing the ways in
which a literary work means while insisting that the
meaning cannot be adequately paraphrased. My approach
in the chapters that follow will make clear my continuing
debt to critics like Cleanth Brooks. But I do not want to
argue, now or later, that the sort of ambiguity I have demonstrated in *The Merchant of Venice* is the ultimate meaning
of all literature, even of all the plays of Shakespeare. In the
rest of this book I shall show how certain kinds of critical
reduction lead us to recognize the particular complexities
of Shakespeare's plays. But the forms of complexity are
not identical with one another, and they constitute not a
celebration of "ambiguity" as the meaning of life but a set
of perceptions of demarcated aspects of existential
complexity.

2

Either/Or: Responding to *Henry V*

Examining *The Merchant of Venice* and its criticism, we contemplated a play which tempts audiences to make sense of it in thematic terms and then, without repudiating those terms, to realize their insufficiency, reductiveness, and troublingly ironic applicability to the play which suggests them. In thus both creating and undermining paraphrasable meaning, in using strategies of ambiguity to make us realize the impossibility of simple solutions to certain kinds of familiar problems on which we nevertheless can and must agree, Shakespeare seems in *The Merchant of Venice* to be demonstrating one peculiar power of art, its ability to mime a world whose principles of coherence are never in doubt but seldom make life as simple as one might expect them to do. I have suggested that a complexity that undercuts thematic paradigms is a constant in Shakespeare's art. I want to propose now, however, that such complexity takes different shapes, to different effect, in different plays. The problem of meaning is not always the same. I shall make my point emphatically by examining another controversial play with a very different kind of critical history from that of *The Merchant of Venice*.

Henry V, too, has repeatedly elicited simple and wholehearted responses from its critics, interpretations that seem solidly based on total readings of a consistent whole. In this instance, however, sophisticated critics have not approached a single consensus; rather, they have gathered into rival camps which could hardly disagree more radically, and one finds two consensus views rather than one. "For some" critics, a recent writer remarks, "the play presents the story of an ideal monarch and glorifies his achievements; for them the tone approaches that of an epic lauding the military virtues. For others, the protagonist is a Machiavellian militarist who professes Christianity but whose deeds reveal both hypocrisy and ruthlessness; for them, the tone is predominantly one of mordant satire."[1]

One way to deal with a play that provokes such conflicting responses is to try to find the truth somewhere between them. Another is to suggest that the dramatist couldn't make up his mind which side he wanted to come down on and left us a mess. A third is to interpret all the signals indicating one polar reading as intentional, and to interpret all the other signals as irrepressible evidence that Shakespeare didn't believe what he was trying to say. All of these strategies have been mounted against *Henry V*. All of them are wrong.

I am going to argue that in *Henry V* Shakespeare created a work whose ultimate power is precisely the fact that it points in two opposite directions, virtually daring us to choose one of the two opposed interpretations it requires of us. In this deceptively simple play Shakespeare experimented, more shockingly than elsewhere, with a structure like the gestaltist's familiar drawing of a rare beast. Gombrich describes the experience of that creature in memorable terms:

> We can see the picture as either a rabbit or a duck. It is easy to discover both readings. It is less easy to describe what happens when we switch from one interpretation to the other. Clearly we do not have the illusion that we are confronted with a "real" duck or rabbit. The shape on the paper resembles neither animal very closely. And yet there is no doubt that the

shape transforms itself in some subtle way when the duck's beak becomes the rabbit's ears and brings an otherwise neglected spot into prominence. I say "neglected," but does it enter our experience at all when we switch back to reading "duck"? To answer this question, we are compelled to look for what is "really there," to see the shape apart from its interpretation, and this, we soon discover, is not really possible. True, we can switch from one reading to another with increasing rapidity; we will also "remember" the rabbit while we see the duck, but the more closely we watch ourselves, the more certainly we will discover that we cannot experience alternative readings at the same time. Illusion, we will find, is hard to describe or analyze, for though we may be intellectually aware of the fact that any given experience *must* be an illusion, we cannot, strictly speaking, watch ourselves having an illusion.[2]

1

If one considers the context of *Henry V,* one realizes that the play could scarcely have been anything but a rabbit-duck.

Henry V is, of course, not only a freestanding play but also the last part of a tetralogy. Some years earlier, when his talent was up to *Titus Andronicus* rather than to *Hamlet,* Shakespeare had had the nerve, at the very beginning of his career, to shape the hopelessly episodic and unstructured materials of his chronicle sources not into the licensed formlessness of the history play his audience was used to—one recalls shapeless domestic chronicles like *Edward I* and *The Famous Victories of King Henry the Fifth* and foreign histories like *Tamburlaine* and *The Battle of Alcazar*—but rather into an integrated series of plays each satisfying as a separate unit but all deriving a degree of added power and meaning from being parts of a unified whole. It is scarcely credible that, with this tetralogy behind him, Shakespeare should have approached the matter of Lancaster without thinking of the possibility of a second unified series of plays. I can think of no other explanation for the fact that already in *Richard II* Hotspur—a character completely unnecessary to that play—has been made practically a generation younger than his model. The implication of the change is that in 1595 Shakespeare already intended a play about Prince Hal. And as one notices the innumerable cross-references and links and parallels among the plays of the second tetralogy, one feels more confidently than in the first cycle that such connections are not afterthoughts, backward indices in one play to what already existed in earlier plays, but evidence of conscious through-composition.

In any event, whether or not, as I think, Shakespeare knew four or five years beforehand that he would write *Henry V*, he certainly did know in 1599 that this drama would be the capstone to an edifice of plays tightly mortared to one another. And as with each part of *Henry IV*, he must have derived enormous power from the expectations his audience brought from the preceding plays. In two of the first three plays the audience had been confronted at the beginning with a set of problems that seemed solved by the end of the preceding play but had erupted in different forms as soon as the new play began. Thus the meaning of each of the plays subsequent to *Richard II* had been enriched by the audience's recognition of the emergence of old problems in a new guise. By the time the cycle reached *Henry V*, the recurrent and interlocking set of problems had become so complex that a reflective audience must have found it impossible to predict how the last play could possibly resolve them.

The unresolved thematic issue at the end of *Richard II* is the conflict of values embodied in the two kings who are its protagonists: Bolingbroke's talent as opposed to Richard's legitimacy; Bolingbroke's extraverted energy and calculating pursuit of power as opposed to Richard's imagination, inwardness, and sense of mortality. Richard's qualities make possible in him a spiritual life that reveals him as closer—even in his inadequacy—to the ideal figures of the comedies than is his successor, who nonetheless has the sheer force to survive and to rule to his country's advantage. If the play is structured to force one by the end to choose Bolingbroke as the better king—one need only contrast his disposition of Exton at the close with Richard's of Mowbray at the opening—one nevertheless finds one's emotions rather surprisingly committed to the failed Richard. *Richard II* thus poses a question that arches over the entire tetralogy: can the manipulative qualities that guarantee political success be combined in one man with the spiritual qualities that make one fully open and responsive to life and therefore fully human? Or, to put it more accurately, can political resourcefulness be combined with qualities more like those of an audience as it sees itself?

1 Henry IV moves the question to a new generation, asking in effect whether the qualities split between Richard and Bolingbroke can be united in Hal. And in the manner of a comedy, it suggests optimistically that indeed they can. Thus Hal's famous schematic stance between the appropriately dead Hotspur and a Falstaff equally appropriately feigning death indicates not so much a compromise between their incompatible values as the difference between Hal's ability to thrive in a world of process by employing time as an instrument and the oddly similar unwillingness of both Hotspur and Falstaff to do so.

For Hotspur, there is only the present moment. Even an hour is too long for life if honor is not its definition, and a self-destructive recklessness leads Hotspur to fight his battle at the wrong time, hoping naively thereby to gain more glory. For Falstaff, time is equally irrelevant. Like the forest of Arden he needs no clock, since he has nowhere to go. He lives cyclically, recurring always to the same satisfactions of the same appetites, playing holiday every day, denying the scars of age and the imminence of death. Both of Hal's alter egos preposterously deny time, Hotspur to meet his death characteristically in midphrase—a phrase that Falstaff has already completed as "Food for powder"—and Falstaff to rise emblematically from his own death and shamelessly assert once again his will to live.

But Hal's affection for both men, so symmetrically expressed, suggests that he is in tune with something in each of them. Unlike his irascible father, but like both Hotspur and Falstaff, he is witty, ebulliently verbal, social, warmly responsive to others. For one illusory moment Shakespeare suggests the possibility of a public man who is privately whole. If the Prince's soliloquy has vowed an amputation he sees from the beginning as necessary, if the play extempore has ended in a suddenly heartbreaking promise to banish plump Jack and banish all the world, followed by the knock of the real world on the door, *1 Henry IV* nevertheless puts us in a comic universe in which Hal need never reject Falstaff in order to reach his father's side in the nick of time; it entices us with the hope of a political world transformed by the life of comedy.

But the end of *Henry IV, Part One* marks only the half-way point, both in this massive tetralogy and in the study of Prince Hal, and *Part Two* brutally denies the comic optimism we might have expected to encounter once again. With the exception of Hotspur, all the ingredients of *Part One* seem to be present again, and in some respects they seem stronger than ever. Falstaff is given a scene (II.iv) perhaps even more endearing than Gadshill and its aftermath; he captivates Doll Tearsheet and, against her better knowledge, the Hostess. Ancient Pistol, who adds fresh attraction to the tavern world, performs one of the functions of the missing Hotspur by giving us a mocking perspective on the rhetoric and pretensions of the warrior.

And yet, despite all this and more, the effect of *Henry IV, Part Two* is to narrow possibilities. The rejection of

Falstaff at its end seems to be both inevitable and right yet
simultaneously seems to darken the world for which the
paradise of the Boar's Head must be lost. Hotspur's ab-
sence, emphasized by the dramatic device of the series of
rumors from which his father must pick it out at the beginning, roots out of the political world the atmosphere of
youth, vigor, charm, and idealistic commitment that
Hotspur almost alone had lent it before. And Hotspur's
widow's just reproaches of her father-in-law stress the old
man's ugly opportunism. Northumberland's nihilistic
curse—

> Let heaven kiss earth! now let not Nature's hand
> Keep the wild flood confin'd! let order die!
> And let this world no longer be a stage
> To feed contention in a ling'ring act;
> But let one spirit of the first-born Cain
> Reign in all bosoms, that each heart being set
> On bloody courses, the rude scene may end,
> And darkness be the burier of the dead! (I.i.153–60)

—makes clear the destructiveness of his rebellion, a thing
far different from his late son's chivalric quest, and it
creates an unequivocal sense that Hal has no choice but to
oppose it as effectively as he can. No longer can we assent
to Falstaff's observation, plausible in *Part One*, that the
rebels "offend none but the virtuous" (III.iii.191), so that
opposing them is almost a game. The harshness of the
rebels' cause and company in *Part Two* demands of the
audience a Hotspurrian recognition that this is no world to
play with mammets and tilt with lips.

Yet the attractiveness of the King's cause is reduced too.
If in some moments—as in his sensitive meditation on the
crown and his emotional final reunion with Hal—Henry
IV is more likable in *Part Two* than he was in *Part One*, he
is no longer an active character (he doesn't even appear
until the third act). And his place is filled by Prince John,
as chilling a character as Shakespeare would ever create.[3]

Either/Or: Responding to *Henry V*

Many a villain has more superficial charm than Hal's up-right brother, and the priggish treachery by which Prince John overcomes the rebels arouses in us a distaste for political action, even when it is necessary, such as no pre-vious moment in the plays has occasioned. If Shrewsbury implied that a mature politics was compatible with the joy of life lived fully and spontaneously, Gaultree now shows political responsibility as masked and sinister, an ally of death.

Given this characterization of the political world as joy-less and cruel, one might expect Falstaff to carry the day. But in fact Shakespeare reduces him as much as he reduces the workaday world. It was a delicate paradox in *Part One* that allowed us to admire Falstaff for his ridiculous denial of mortality—"They hate us youth"; "young men must live." Falstaff might worry about how he was dwindling away, but we had no fear of losing so eternal a companion. Or, to put it more accurately, we loved him for allaying such fears; for all his grumbling at Gadshill, he could run when he had to. But in *Part Two,* Falstaff is mired in gross physicality and the ravages of age, obsessed with his dis-eases and bodily functions, commanding that the jordan be emptied, confirming as Doll caresses him ("I am old, I am old") his stage audience's observation that desire has out-lasted performance. He is the same Falstaff, but the bal-ance is altered.

As if for the reenactment of his great catechism on honor in *Part One,* Falstaff is given a similar aria in *Part Two.* But the praise of sherris sack, funny as it is, is no more than a witty paean to alcohol, and a description at that of the mechanical operation of the spirit, whereas the rejection of honor in *Part One* was convincing enough almost to undo our respect for anyone who subordinates life to ideals. Or again, the charge of foot for whom Falstaff is responsible in *Part One* never becomes palpable, except to elicit his sympathetic "Food for powder," which puts him essentially on their side. In *Part Two,* however, we are introduced to his men by name, we see him choosing them (for the most self-serving reasons), and we are aware of the lives and families that Falstaff is ruining. No longer can we see him as the spokesman of life for its own sake; his ego is opportunistic, as not before, at the expense of others.

If the tavern world is no longer alluring for us, it is even more unattractive for Hal. Physically separated from Falstaff in *Part Two* as not in *Part One,* the Prince is ready at any moment to express his discomfort, his guilt, his eagerness to be away. The flyting he carries on with Poins is unpleasant: if Hal feels so out of place consorting with commoners, why doesn't he simply stop doing it? We are tempted to agree with Warwick, who tells the King that Hal's only reason for spending time with his companions is his opportunistic scheme to use them:

> The Prince but studies his companions
> Like a strange tongue, where, to gain the language,
> 'Tis needful that the immodest word
> Be look'd upon and learnt, which once attain'd,
> Your Highness knows, comes to no further use
> But to be known and hated. (IV.iv.68–73)

The diseases literally corrupting Falstaff's body are endemic in *2 Henry IV.* Sickness and death pervade every element of the plot, virtually every scene, and it is no accident that it is here, not in *Part One,* that we meet Justice Shallow, in senile debility only a step beyond the aged helplessness of Northumberland and the King. If the medium of action in *Part One* was time seen as a hidden road that leads providentially toward a fulfilling moment, the medium of *Part Two* is repetitious and meaningless process drawing relentlessly to universal annihilation. Could one "read the book of fate," the moribund King reflects, one would have to

> see the revolution of the times
> Make mountains level, and the continent,

> Weary of solid firmness, melt itself
> Into the sea, and other times to see
> The beachy girdle of the ocean
> Too wide for Neptune's hips. (III.i.45–51)

What we recognize here is the time of the sonnets, of Ecclesiastes; and Warwick can cheer the King only by reminding him that at least time is inevitable. The sickness that infects both Falstaff and the body politic is the sickness of life itself, joyless and rushing to the grave. In such a world Prince Hal cannot play. He must do what he can for his kingdom, and that means casting Falstaff aside.

About the necessity for the rejection we are not given the chance to have any doubts: Falstaff, after all, has just told his companions that the law is his now, and, as A. R. Humphreys notes, Richard II had assured his own fall by making precisely this Nixonian claim.[4] Yet we are forced to feel, and painfully, what an impoverishment of Hal's life the rejection causes.[5] And we recognize another aspect of that impoverishment in the drive that moves Hal to take the crown prematurely from his dying father: his commitment to political power has impelled him, as the King recognizes bitterly, to a symbolic gesture that reveals an unconscious readiness for parricide. At the end of *Henry IV, Part One,* Hal seemed able to accommodate all of England into his family as he moved toward its symbolic fatherhood. By the end of *Part Two,* in order to become king of England he has reached out to murder both of his fathers.

2

If we fancy ourselves arriving, on an afternoon in 1599, for the first performance of *Henry V,* we must imagine ourselves quite unsure of what to expect. Some months earlier the Epilogue to *2 Henry IV* had promised that "our humble author will continue the story, with Sir John in it, and make you merry with fair Katherine of France, where (for any thing I know) Falstaff shall die of a sweat, unless already 'a be kill'd with your hard opinions; for Oldcastle died [a] martyr, and this is not the man." This disingenuous come-on allows for both sympathetic and hostile readings of Falstaff, while disclaiming any knowledge of the author's intentions. But the plays that precede *Henry V* have aroused such ambivalent expectations that the question of the Epilogue is trivial. If *Henry V* had followed directly on *1 Henry IV,* we might have expected to be made merry by the comedy such critics as Dover Wilson have taken that play to be,[6] for we have seen a Hal potentially larger than his father, possessing the force that politics requires without the sacrifice of imagination and range that Bolingbroke has had to pay. But *Part Two* has told us that *Part One* deceived us, for the day has had to come when Hal, no longer able to live in two worlds, would be required to make his choice, and the Prince has had to expel from his life the very qualities that made him better than his father. Have we not, after *Part Two,* good reason to expect in the play about Hal's kingship the study of an opportunist who has traded his humanity for his success, covering over the ruthlessness of the politician with the mere appearance of fellowship that his past has endowed him with? Surely this is what Goddard means when he calls Henry V "the golden casket of *The Merchant of Venice,* fairer to a superficial view than to a more searching perception."[7]

As we watch the Chorus stride across the stage of the Curtain theater, then, we are ready for one of two opposed presentations of the reign of the fifth Henry. Perhaps we hope that the play now beginning will resolve our doubts, set us right, give us a single gestalt to replace the antithetical images before our mind's eye. And that, as is demonstrated by the unequivocal interpretations good critics continue to make, is exactly the force of the play. We are made to see a rabbit or a duck. In fact, if we do not try obsessively to cling to memories of past encounters with the play, we may find that each time we read it it turns from one shape to the other, just as it so regularly does in production. I want to show that *Henry V* is brilliantly capable of being read, fully and subtly, as each of the plays the two parts of *Henry IV* had respectively anticipated. Leaving the theater at the end of the first performance, some members of the audience knew that they had seen a rabbit, others a duck. Still others, and I would suggest that they were Shakespeare's best audience, knew uneasily that they did not know what to think.

3
———————

Think of *Henry V* as an extension of *1 Henry IV*. For the generation who came to know it under the spell of Olivier's great film, it is hard to imagine *Henry V* any other way, but Olivier's distortions, deletions, and embellishments only emphasized what is already in the play. The structure of the entire cycle has led from the beginning of conflict in a quarrel to its end in a wedding, from the disruption of royal power to its unchallenged reassertion. If *Richard II* at the beginning transformed the normally episodic chronicle form into tragedy, *Henry V* at the end turns it into comedy: the plot works through the troubles of a threatening world to end in marriage and the promise of a green world. Its protagonist, like Benedick returned to Messina, puts aside military exploits for romance, and charms even his enemies with his effervescent young manhood. Its prologue insists, as the comedies always do, on the importance of imagination, a faculty which Bolingbroke, wise to the needs of a tragic world, had rejected in *Richard II* as dangerous. And, as in all romantic comedy, providence guides the play's events to their desired conclusion.[8]

   To be sure, Olivier's camera and Walton's music prettied up the atmosphere, transporting their war-weary audience to the fairy-tale world of the Duc de Berry. But they found their cues in the play—in the Chorus's epic romanticizations of land and sea, his descriptions of festooned fleets and nocturnal campfires and eager warriors, and his repeated invitations to imagine even more and better. Nor did Olivier invent his film's awe at the spectacle of the past. In *Henry V,* as nowhere before in the tetralogy, Shakespeare excites us by making us conscious that we are privileged to be watching the very moments at which event transforms itself into history:

> MONT.   The day is yours.
> K. HEN. Praised be God, and not our strength, for it!
>   What is this castle call'd that stands hard by?
> MONT. They call it Agincourt.
> K. HEN. Then call we this the field of Agincourt,
>   Fought on the day of Crispin Crispianus.
>   (IV.vii.86–91)

Ultimately, it was not Olivier's pictures but the play's language that made his *Henry V* so overwhelming; the rhetoric of the play is extraordinary, unprecedented even in Shakespeare. Think, for example, of the King's oration to his troops on Saint Crispin's day (IV.iii.19–67). Thematically, of course, the speech is a tour de force, subjecting motifs from the tetralogy to Aeschylean transmutations. Like the dying John of Gaunt, Harry is inspired by a vision of England, but one characteristically his own, made as romantic by the fantasy of neighborhood legionnaires and domestic history lessons as by the magical names of England's leaders. Unlike Richard II, Harry disprizes trappings, "outward things." Like Hotspur, he cares only about honor and wants to fight with as few troops as possible in order to acquire more of it: "the fewer men, the greater share of honor." Like Falstaff, he is finicky about the kind of men he adventures with: "we would not die in that man's company / That fears his fellowship to die with us." Again like Falstaff, he thinks of the "flowing cups" to come when the day's work is done, and sees the day's events in festival terms. Gaily doing battle on the feast of

Crispian, he is literally playing at war like Hotspur, paradoxically uniting the opposed principles of the two most enchanting characters of the cycle.

Such echoes and allusions give Henry's speech a satisfying finality, a sense of closure. He is the man we have been waiting for, the embodiment of all the virtues the cycle has made us prize, without the vices that had accompanied them before. "He is as full of valor as of kindness," we have heard just before the speech, "Princely in both," and the Crispin's day exhortation demonstrates precisely the combination of attributes that Sherman Hawkins has pointed out as belonging to the ideal monarch postulated by Elizabethan royalism.[9] But even more powerful than its thematic content is the stunning rhetoric of the King's tirade: its movement from the King's honor to his people's; its crescendo variations on Saint Crispin's day, reaching their climax in the last line; its rhythmic patterns expanding repeatedly from broken lines to flowing periods in each section and concluding climactically in the coda that begins "We happy few"; its language constantly addressed to the pleasures, worries, and aspirations of an audience of citizens. As Michael Goldman perceptively argues, such a speech almost literally moves us. We recognize it as a performance; we share the strain of the King's greatness, the necessary effort of his image-projecting. "We are thrilled," Goldman says, "because he is brilliantly meeting a political challenge that has been spelled out for us. . . . It is a moment when he must respond to the unspoken needs of his men, and we respond to his success as we do when a political leader we admire makes a great campaign speech: we love him for his effectiveness."[10]

The fourth act of *Henry V,* in the third scene of which this speech has its place, is a paradigm of the King's virtues. It begins with the Chorus's contrast between the "confident and over-lusty French" and the thoughtful and patient Englishmen at their watchful fires on the eve of Agincourt, visited by their generous, loving, brave, and concerned royal captain—"a little touch of Harry in the night." The act moves, first through contrasting scenes in the two camps, then through confrontations of various sorts between the opposing sides, to the victory at Agincourt and the King's call for the charitable treatment of the dead as he announces his return to England. In the course of the act we see Harry, constantly contrasted to the stupid and corrupt French, in a triumphant show of bravery and high spirits. But we see him also in a kind of inwardness we have seldom observed in his father, listening as neither Richard II nor Henry IV could have done to the complaints and fears of a common soldier who knows what kings impose on their subjects that the kings themselves do not have to risk. His reponse is a soliloquy as powerful in its thematic and rhetorical complexity as the public address we have just considered (IV.i.230–84).

In some respects this soliloquy, which precedes by only a few moments the Crispin's day speech, is the thematic climax of the entire tetralogy, showing us that at last we have a king free of the crippling disabilities of his predecessors and wise in what the plays have been teaching. Recognizing that all that separates a king from private men is ceremony, Harry has escaped Richard's tragic confusion of ceremony with reality: "Is not the King's name twenty thousand names?" Unwittingly reenacting his father's insomniac soliloquy in the third act of *2 Henry IV*, Harry too longs for the heart's ease of the commoner. But where the old King could conclude only, "Uneasy lies the head that wears a crown," recurring despairingly to his posture of perennial guiltiness and to his weary sense of mortality, his young son ends by remembering his responsibility, his life of service, and sees that—"what watch the King keeps to maintain the peace"—as the defining mark of the king. Moreover, in his catechistic questioning of ceremony Harry shows that he has incorporated Falstaff's clearsightedness: like honor in Falstaff's catechism, ceremony consists only in what is conferred by others, bringing no tangible good to its bearer, unable to cure disease, no more than a proud dream. But the lesson is not only Falstaff's; for, at the opposite end of the tetralogy, before Hal ever entered the scene, a young Bolingbroke had anticipated his son's "Thinks thou the fiery fever will go out / With titles blown from adulation?" with a similar repudiation of comforting self-deception:

> O, who can hold a fire in his hand
> By thinking of the frosty Caucasus?
> Or cloy the hungry edge of appetite
> By bare imagination of a feast?
> (Richard II, I.iii.294–97)

These multiple allusions force us to see in Henry V the epitome of what the cycle has taught us to value as best in a monarch, indeed in a man; and the King's ability to listen to the soldier Williams and to hear him suggests, like his subsequent fooling with Fluellen in the same fourth act, a king who is fully a man. All that is needed to complete him is mature sexuality, scarcely hinted at in the earlier portraits of Hal, and the wooing of Princess Katherine in the fifth act brings finality to a lively portrayal of achieved manhood, a personality integrated in itself and ready to bring unity and joy to a realm that has suffered long from rule by men less at ease with themselves and less able to identify their own interests with those of their country.[11] It was such a response to *Henry V* that led me years ago to write:

> In only one play in his entire career does Shakespeare seem bent on making us believe that what is valuable in politics and in life can successfully be combined in a ruler as in his state. . . . There can be no doubt that [the play] is infectiously patriotic, or that the ideal of the harmonious commonweal . . . reflects the highest point of Shakespeare's civic optimism. And Henry is clearly presented as the kind of exemplary monarch that neither Richard II nor Hen-

ry IV could be, combining the inwardness and the
sense of occasion of the one and the strength of the
other with a generous humanity available to
neither. . . . In *Henry V* Shakespeare would have us
believe what hitherto his work in its genre has denied,
that in the real world of the chronicles a man may live
who embodies the virtues and experiences the fortunes of the comic hero.[12]

Reading the play thus optimistically, I had to note
nevertheless how many readers respond otherwise to it,
and I went on to observe that the play casts so many dark
shadows—on England after Agincourt, for instance—that
one can scarcely share its optimism, and that "in this respect *Henry V* is the most melancholy of the history plays."
But I have now come to believe that my acknowledgment
of that darker aspect of the play hardly suggested the terrible subversiveness with which Shakespeare undermines
the entire structure.

4

Taking the play, as we have just done, to be an extension
of the first part of *Henry IV,* we are almost inevitably pro-
pelled to optimism. Taking it as the sequel of the second
part of *Henry IV,* we are led to the opposite view held by
critics as diverse as H. C. Goddard, Roy W. Battenhouse,
Mark Van Doren, and H. M. Richmond. Think of those
dark shadows that cloud the comedy. The point of the
stock ending of romantic comedy is, of course, its guarantee of the future: marriage secures and reinvigorates society while promising an extension of its happiness into a
generation to come. Like *A Midsummer Night's Dream,*
Henry V ends in a marriage whose blessing will transform
the world:

K. HEN. Now welcome, Kate; and bear me witness
all,

That here I kiss her as my sovereign queen. *Flourish.*
Q. ISA. God, the best maker of all marriages,
Combine your hearts in one, your realms in one!
As man and wife, being two, are one in love,
So be there 'twixt your kingdoms such a spousal,
That never may ill office, or fell jealousy,
Which troubles oft the bed of blessed marriage,
Thrust in between the [paction] of these kingdoms,
To make divorce of their incorporate league;
That English may as French, French Englishmen,
Receive each other. God speak this Amen!
   ALL. Amen!
   K. HEN. Prepare we for our marriage; on which day,
My Lord of Burgundy, we'll take your oath,
And all the peers', for surety of our leagues.
Then shall I swear to Kate, and you to me,
And may our oaths well kept and prosp'rous be!
                              Sennet. Exeunt.

We don't really know very much about what was to
happen in Theseus's Athens. Be we know a good deal
about Plantagenet England; and in case any member of the
audience has forgotten a history as familiar to Elizabethans
as our Civil War is to us, the Chorus appears immediately
to remind them—both of what would soon happen, and of
the fact that they have already seen a cycle of Shakespearean plays presenting that dismal story. The shock of
the suddenly depressing reversal of all the optimism
suggested by the first ending is all the more intense because the Chorus's speech promises in its opening lines to
continue in the celebratory vein of the last scene, only to
turn unexpectedly in its last four lines to harsh negation:

Small time, but in that small most greatly lived
This star of England. Fortune made his sword;
By which the world's best garden he achieved,
And of it left his son imperial lord.
Henry the Sixt, in infant bands crown'd King

> Of France and England, did this king succeed;
> Whose state so many had the managing,
> That they lost France, and made his England bleed;
> Which oft our stage hath shown; and for their sake,
> In your fair minds let this acceptance take.[13]

"But if the cause be not good," Williams muses on the eve of Agincourt (IV.i.134–42), "the King himself hath a heavy reckoning to make, when all those legs and arms, and heads, chopp'd off in a battle, shall join together at the latter day and cry all, 'We died at such a place'—some swearing, some crying for a surgeon, some upon their wives left poor behind them, some upon the debts they owe, some upon their children rawly left. I am afeard there are few die well that die in a battle." Replying to Williams, the King insists that the state of a man's soul at the moment of his death is his own responsibility. Though to Samuel Johnson this appeared "a very just distinction,"[14] the King's answer evades the issue: the suffering he is capable of inflicting, the necessity of being sure that the burden is imposed for a worthy cause. The end of the play bleakly implies that there is no such cause; all that Harry has won will be lost within a generation. The Epilogue wrenches us out of the paradise of comedy into the purgatory of Shakespearean time, where we incessantly watch

> the hungry ocean gain
> Advantage on the kingdom of the shore,
> And the firm soil win of the wat'ry main,
> Increasing store with loss, and loss with store.

Contemplation of "such interchange of state, / Or state itself confounded to decay" (Sonnet 64) does not incline one toward attempting apocalyptic action. It is more likely to encourage reflections like those of Henry IV about the "revolution of the times," or of Falstaff in the very next scene of *2 Henry IV:* "let time shape, and there an end" (III.ii.332).

But the implication that the cause is not good disturbs us well before the aftermath of Agincourt. The major justification for the war is the Archbishop of Canterbury's harangue on the Salic law governing hereditary succession, a law the French are said to have violated. The Archbishop's speech to the King follows immediately on his announcement to the Bishop of Ely that he plans to propose the war as a means of alleviating a financial crisis in the church. The speech itself is long, legalistic, peppered with exotic genealogies impossible to follow; its language is involuted and syntactically loose. The very qualities that make its equivalent in Shakespeare's sources an unexceptionable instrument of statecraft make it sound on the stage like doubletalk, and Canterbury's conclusion that it is "as clear as is the summer's sun" that King Henry is legitimate king of France is a sardonic bit of comedy.[15] Olivier, unwilling to let on that Shakespeare might want us to be less than convinced, turned the episode into farce at the expense of the Elizabethan actor playing the part of Canterbury. Denied the resources of a subsidized film industry, scholars who want to see the war justified must praise the speech on the basis of its content, ignoring its length and style. Thus in the words of one scholar, "the Archbishop discharges his duty faithfully, as it stands his reasoning is impeccable apart from any warrant given by the precedent of Edward III's claims. Henry is not initiating aggression."[16] Bradley, whose argument the critic just cited was answering, is truer to the situation: "Just as he went to war chiefly because, as his father told him, it was the way to keep factious nobles quiet and unite the nation, so when he adjures the Archbishop to satisfy him as to his right to the French throne, he knows very well that the Archbishop *wants* the war, because it will defer and perhaps prevent what he considers the spoliation of the Church."[17]

J. H. Walter points out that Henry's reaction to the insulting gift of tennis balls from the Dauphin is strategically placed, as not in the play's sources, after the King has already decided to go to war, and he argues that Shakespeare thus "uses [the incident] to show Henry's christian self-control."[18] This is an odd description of a speech which promises to avenge the gift with the griefs of "many a thousand widows" for their husbands, of mothers for their sons, and even of "some [who] are yet ungotten and unborn" (I.ii.284–87). Since the tennis balls are a response to a challenge already issued (Henry's claim that France is his by rights) the King's rage seems just a little self-righteous. Henry's insistence throughout the scene that the Archbishop reassure him as to his right to make the claim insures our suspicion that the war is not quite the selfless enterprise other parts of the play tempt us to see.

Our suspicions are deepened by what happens later. H. C. Goddard has left us a devastating attack on Henry V as Shakespeare's model Machiavellian.[19] Goddard's intemperate analysis, as right as it is one-sided, should be read by everyone interested in the play. I want to quote only one brief excerpt, his summary of the "five scenes devoted to" the battle of Agincourt; the account will be particularly useful to those who remember the battle scenes in Olivier's film.

1. Pistol captures a Frenchman.

2. The French lament their everlasting shame at being worsted by slaves.

3. Henry weeps at the deaths of York and Suffolk and orders every soldier to kill his prisoners.

4. Fluellen compares Henry with Alexander and his rejection of Falstaff to the murder of Cleitus. Henry, entering angry, swears that every French prisoner, present and future, shall have his throat cut. . . . The battle is over. The King prays God to keep him honest and breaks his word of honor to Williams.

5. Henry offers Williams money by way of satisfaction, which Williams rejects. Word is brought that

10,000 French are slain and 29 English. Henry gives the victory to God.

If Shakespeare had deliberately set out to deglorify the Battle of Agincourt in general and King Henry in particular it would seem as if he could hardly have done more.[20]

Admittedly, Goddard's analysis is excessively partisan. He ignores the rhetoric we have admired, he sees only the King's hypocrisy on Agincourt eve, and he refuses the Chorus's repeated invitations to view the war as more glorious than what is shown. But the burden of Goddard's argument is difficult to set aside: the war scenes reinforce the unpleasant implications of the Salic law episode. Consider the moment, before the great battle, when the King bullies the citizens of Harfleur, whose surrender he demands, with a rapacious violence that even J. H. Walter does not cite as an instance of "Henry's christian self-control":

> If I begin the batt'ry once again,
> I will not leave the half-achieved Harflew
> Till in her ashes she lies buried.
> The gates of mercy shall be all shut up,
> And the flesh'd soldier, rough and hard of heart,
> In liberty of bloody hand, shall range
> With conscience wide as hell, mowing like grass
> Your fresh fair virgins and your flow'ring infants.
> What is it then to me, if impious War,
> Arrayed in flames like to the prince of fiends,
> Do with his smirch'd complexion all fell feats
> Enlink'd to waste and desolation?
> What is't to me, when you yourselves are cause,
> If your pure maidens fall into the hand
> Of hot and forcing violation?
> What reign can hold licentious wickedness
> When down the hill he holds his fierce career?
>
> (III.iii.7–23)

In such language as Tamburlaine styled his "working words," the King, like the kind of aggressor we know all too well, blames the rapine he solicits on his victims. The alacrity of his attack makes one understand Yeats's description of Henry V as "a ripened Fortinbras"; its sexual morbidity casts a disquieting light on the muted but unmistakable aggressiveness of his sexual assault on Katherine in the fifth act.

Henry's killing of the French prisoners inspires similar uneasiness. Olivier justified this violation of the putative ethics of war by making it a response to the French killing of the English luggage boys, and one of the most moving moments of his film was the King's passionate response: "I was not angry since I came to France / Until this instant." After such a moment one could hardly fault Henry's

> Besides, we'll cut the throats of those we have,
> And not a man of them that we shall take
> Shall taste our mercy. (IV.vii.55–65)

In the same scene, indeed, Gower observes that it was in response to the slaughter of the boys that "the King, most worthily, hath caus'd every soldier to cut his prisoner's throat. O, 'tis a gallant king!" But the timing is wrong: Gower's announcement came *before* the King's touching speech. In fact, Shakespeare had presented the decision to kill the prisoners as made at the end of the preceding scene, and while in the source it has a strategic point, in the play it is simply a response to the fair battlefield killing of some English nobles by the French. Thus the announcement comes twice, first as illegitimate, second as if it were a spontaneous outburst of forgivable passion when it actually is not. In such moments as this we feel an eloquent discrepancy between the glamor of the play's rhetoric and the reality of its action.

Henry IV, Part One is "about temperance and fortitude," *Part Two* is "about wisdom and justice," and Shakespeare's "plan culminates in *Henry V*." So argues Sherman Hawkins.[21] "Henry's right to France—and by implication England—," he claims, "is finally vindicated by a higher power than the Archbishop of Canterbury."[22] God's concern that France be governed by so ideal a monarch culminates, of course, in the ruins so movingly described in Act V by the Duke of Burgundy, to whose plea the King responds like the leader of a nation of shopkeepers with a demand that France "buy [the] peace" it wants according to a contract Henry just happens to have had drawn up. What follows is the King's coarse wooing of his captive princess, with its sexual innuendo, its repeated gloating over Henry's possession of the realm for which he sues, and its arch insistence on his sudden lack of adequate rhetoric. Johnson's judgment is hardly too severe: the King "has neither the vivacity of Hal nor the grandeur of Henry. ...We have here but a mean dialogue for princes; the merriment is very gross, and the sentiments are very worthless."[23]

Henry's treatment of France may suggest to the irreverent that one is better off when providence does not supply such a conqueror. And his impact on England is scarcely more salubrious. The episodes in which the King tricks Fluellen and terrifies Williams recall the misbehavior of the old Hal, but with none of the old charm and a lot more power to do hurt. In *2 Henry IV* it was the unspeakable Prince John who dealt self-righteously with traitors; in *Henry V* it is the King himself. In the earlier plays wars were begun by others; in *Henry V* it is the King himself, as he acknowledges in his soliloquy, having apparently decided not to go on pinning the blame on the Archbishop of Canterbury. And England must pay a high price for the privilege of the returning veterans to show their wounds every October 25.

We do no have to wait for the Epilogue to get an idea of it. At the end of Act IV, as we saw, the King calls for holy rites for the dead and orders a return to England. The Chorus to the ensuing act invites us to imagine the King's triumphant return, his modesty, and the outpouring of grateful citizens. But in the next scene we find ourselves still in France, where Fluellen gives Pistol, last of the company of the Boar's Head, the comeuppance he has long fended off with his shield of preposterous language. Forced to eat his leek, Pistol mutters one last imprecation ("all hell shall stir for this"), listens to Gower's final tongue-lashing, and, alone on the stage at last, speaks in soliloquy:

> Doth Fortune play the huswife with me now?
> News have I that my Doll is dead i' th' spittle
> Of a malady of France.
> And there my rendezvous is quite cut off.
> Old do I wax, and from my weary limbs
> Honor is cudgell'd. Well, bawd I'll turn,
> And something lean to cutpurse of quick hand.
> To England will I steal, and there I'll steal;
> And patches will I get unto these cudgell'd scars,
> And [swear] I got them in the Gallia wars. (V.i.80–89)

The pun on "steal" is the last faint echo of the great Falstaff scenes, but labored and lifeless now as Pistol's pathetic bravura. Pistol's *Exit* occasioned Johnson's most affecting critical comment: "The comick scenes of the history of Henry the Fourth and Fifth are now at an end, and all the comick personages are now dismissed. Falstaff and Mrs. Quickly are dead; Nym and Bardolph are hanged; Gadshill was lost immediately after the robbery; Poins and Peto have vanished since, one knows not how; and Pistol is now beaten into obscurity. I believe every reader regrets their departure."[24] But our regret is for more than the end of some high comedy: it is for the reality of the postwar world the play so powerfully conjures up—soldiers returned home to find their jobs gone, falling to a life of crime in a seamy and impoverished underworld that scarcely remembers the hopes that accompanied the beginnings of the adventure.

It is the "duty of the ruler," Hawkins says, "to make his subjects good."[25] For the failure of his subjects, the play tells us, we must hold Henry V and his worthless war responsible. Unsatisfactory though he was, Henry IV was still the victim of the revolution of the times, and our ultimate attitude toward him, hastened to death as he was by the unconscious ambition of his own son, took a sympathetic turn like that with which we came at the end to regard the luckless Richard. But Henry V, master manipulator of time, has by the end of the cycle immersed himself in the destructive element. The blows he has rained on his country are much more his than those of any enemy of the people, and all he has to offer his bleeding subjects for the few years that remain is the ceremonial posture which he himself has earlier had the insight to contemn. Like the Edmund of *King Lear,* another lusty and manipulative warrior who wins, woos, and dies young, Henry might have subscribed himself "in the ranks of death."

5

This, then, is the problem of *Henry V*. Along the way I have cited some critics who see an exemplary Christian monarch, one who has attained, "in the language of Ephesians, both the 'age' and 'stature' of a perfect man."[26] And I have cited others who see "the perfect Machiavellian prince,"[27] a coarse and brutal highway robber.[28] Despite their obvious differences, these rival views are essentially similar, for each sees only a clear gestalt. I hope that simply by juxtaposing the two readings I have shown that each of them, persuasive as it may be, is reductive, requiring that we exclude too much to hold it.

Other positions, as I suggested at the outset, are possible. One of them began with Samuel Johnson, was developed by some of the best critics of a generation ago, among them Tillyard and Van Doren, and found its most

humane expression in a fine essay in which Una Ellis-
Fermor argued that by 1599 Shakespeare no longer be-
lieved what he found himself committed to create.[29] Having achieved his portrait of the exemplary public man, she
suggests, Shakespeare was already on the verge of a series
of plays that would ever more vexingly question the virtue
of such virtue. Never again would Shakespeare ask us to
sympathize with a successful politician, instead relegating
such men to the distasteful roles of Fortinbras, Octavius
(in both *Julius Caesar* and *Antony and Cleopatra*),
Alcibiades, and Aufidius. Malcolm is a terrible crux in
Macbeth. Between quarto and folio texts of *Lear*, Shakespeare or his redactor is unable to devote enough attention to the surviving ruler of Britain for us to be able to
identify him confidently. The governance of Cyprus and
Venice is a slighter concern in *Othello* than the embroidery
on the Moor's handkerchief. "Not even Shakespeare,"
Johnson said of what he considered the failure of the last
act of *Henry V,* "can write well without a proper subject. It
is a vain endeavor for the most skilful hand to cultivate
barrenness, or to paint upon vacuity."[30]

A. P. Rossiter's seminal essay, "Ambivalence—the Dialectic of the Histories," sensitively shows Shakespeare's
double view of every important issue in the earlier history
plays. But when he comes to *Henry V,* Rossiter abandons
his schema and decides that Shakespeare momentarily lost
his interest in a problematic view of reality and settled for
shallow propaganda on behalf of a character whom already
he knew well enough to loathe.[31] But *Henry V* is too good
a play for criticism to go on calling it a failure. It has been
performed successfully with increasing frequency in recent
years, and critics have been treating it with increasing
respect.

A third response has been suggested by some writers of
late: *Henry V* is a subtle and complex study of a king who
curiously combines strengths and weaknesses, virtues and
vices.[32] One is attracted to the possibility of regarding the

play unpolemically. Shakespeare is not often polemical, after all, and a balanced view allows for the inclusion of both positive and negative features in an analysis of the protagonist and the action. But sensitive as such analysis can be, it is oddly unconvincing, for two strong reasons. First, the cycle has led us to expect stark answers to simple and urgent questions. Is a particular king good or bad for England? Can one be a successful public man and retain a healthy inner life? Has Hal lost or gained in the transformation through which he changes name and character? Does political action confer any genuine benefit on the polity? What is honor worth, and who has it? The mixed view of Henry characteristically appears in critical essays that seem to fudge such questions, to see complication and subtlety where Shakespeare's art forces us to demand commitment, resolution, answers. Second, no real compromise is possible between the extreme readings I have claimed the play provokes. Our experience of the play resembles the experience Gombrich claims for viewers of the trick drawing: "We can switch from one reading to another with increasing rapidity; we will also 'remember' the rabbit while we see the duck, but the more closely we watch ourselves, the more certainly we will discover that we cannot experience alternative readings at the same time."

6

What I have been describing in *Henry V* sounds very much like what Empson seems to announce in his seventh type of ambiguity, though as usual he is talking about words rather than about anything so grand as a whole play:

> An example of the seventh type of ambiguity . . . occurs when the two meanings of the word, the two values of the ambiguity, are the two opposite meanings defined by the context, so that the total effect is to show a fundamental division in the writer's mind.[33]

If what happens in *Henry V* is a version of the fundamental ambiguity that many critics have found at the center of the Shakespeare vision,[34] it is nevertheless significantly different here. Such ambiguity is not a theme or even the most important fact in many plays in which it figures. I have argued elsewhere that it is extraordinarily important in *Hamlet,* but to reduce *Hamlet* to a statement about "complementarity" is to remove its life.[35] Though one perceives it informing plays as different from one another as *A Midsummer Night's Dream* and *King Lear,* one cannot say that it is what they are "about," and readings of Shakespearean plays as communicating only ambiguity are as arid as readings in which the plays are seen to be about appearance and reality; just so in Empson ambiguity often seems to be merely a trope, a stock tool in the poet's kit.

In *Henry V,* however, Shakespeare's habitual recognition of the irreducible complexity of things has led him, as it should lead his audience, to a point of crisis. Since by now virtually every other play in the canon has been called a problem play, let me add *Henry V* to the number. Suggesting the necessity of radically opposed responses to a historical figure about whom there would seem to have been little reason for anything but the simplest of views, Shakespeare leaves us at a loss. Is it any wonder that *Julius Caesar* would follow in a few months, where Shakespeare would present one of the defining moments in world history in such a way that his audience cannot determine whether the protagonist is the best or the worst of men, whether the central action springs from disinterested idealism or vainglorious egotism, whether that action is virtuous and necessary or wicked and gratuitous? Nor is one surprised to see that the most romantic and comic of Shakespeare's history plays was created at the moment when he was about to abandon romantic comedy, poised for flight into the greater tragedies with their profounder questions about the meaning of action and heroism. The clash between the two possible views of *Henry V* suggests a spiritual struggle in Shakespeare that he would spend the rest of his career working through. One sees a similar oscillation, magnified and reemphasized, in the problem plays and tragedies, and one is tempted to read the romances as a last profound effort to reconcile the irreconcilable. The terrible fact about *Henry V* is that Shakespeare seems equally tempted by both its rival gestalts. And he forces us, as we experience and reexperience and reflect on the play, as we encounter it in performances which inevitably lean in one direction or the other, to share his conflict.

Henry V is most valuable for us not because it points to a crisis in Shakespeare's spiritual life, but because it shows us something about ourselves: the simultaneity of our deepest hopes and fears about the world of political action. In this play, Shakespeare reveals the conflicts between the private selves with which we are born and the public selves we must become, between our longing that authority figures be like us and our suspicion that they must have traded away their inwardness for the sake of power. The play contrasts our hope that society can solve our problems with our knowledge that society has never done so. The inscrutability of *Henry V* is the inscrutability of history. And for a unique moment in Shakespeare's work ambiguity is the heart of the matter, the single most important fact we must confront in plucking out the mystery of the world we live in.

3

Tragic Meanings:
The Redactor as Critic

Examining a comedy and a history in the light of recent criticism, we have noticed two phenomena: on the one hand plays whose effect depends heavily on kinds of complexity that resist interpretative simplification, and on the other critical approaches so frequently inclined to reduction that one must recognize the impulse to simplify as an authentic part of the plays' action on an audience. The regular critical illumination of certain features of these plays, as we have seen, has silhouetted other essential features. In each case the attempt to reduce the play to a thematic paradigm has enabled us to locate the source of the play's significant and irreducible multivalence. At the same time, as I suggested earlier (pp. 19–22), our dual focus has told us something about the critical enterprise and its relation to the world from which it comes. The value put on thematic straightforwardness even by critics whose sensibility and responsiveness demonstrably resist it points up the rational aspiration of much of the critical enterprise: thematic criticism makes literature and itself part of modern intellectual life by making plays seem cognitively clearer and simpler than they are.

I propose to turn now to another kind of play and to a very different kind of criticism where once again an extraordinary agreement among critics as to what they want to simplify will tell us something about the meaning of their undertaking while, more importantly, isolating and illuminating vital qualities of the plays. The plays we shall be looking at are a group of Shakespeare's tragedies, from almost the beginning to the end of his years as tragedian. The critical versions are not what one normally thinks of as criticism. Rather, they are a series of Restoration imitations and adaptations of the tragedies, selected from the many that audiences applauded for the century and more after the return of monarchy to England. Some of these adaptations—Tate's *King Lear,* for example—are well known and widely discussed, though critics have often failed to come to terms either with their essential shrewdness in making Shakespeare into something else or with what they tell us about the originals. Others—Davenant's *Macbeth,* for example—are less widely studied, and equally instructive. Still others, the imitations, point in the same direction as the actual revisions. One of the two I intend to discuss, Dryden's *All for Love,* is inevitably held up against the play it imitates, though not always on the right grounds; the other, Otway's *Venice Preserved,* has not been recognized, as I think its author intended it to be recognized, as an imitation of a particular Shakespearean tragedy. Taken together, these imitations and adaptations constitute a singularly univocal reading of the tragedies. Set against them, the tragedies, different as they are from one another, will reveal crucial aspects of their own quiddity.

1

I shall speak presently of the adaptations, but I want to begin with two improvisatory imitations of Shakespeare that are often claimed to be the best tragedies of their period: *All for Love* and *Venice Preserved.* The ritual gesture in discussing *All for Love* is to observe that the play is best understood not as an attempt to redo or compete with Shakespeare but rather as the culmination of Dryden's career in tragedy. Because we may fully appreciate the remarkable power of *All for Love* only by refraining from measuring it against its predecessor, there is much to be said for this gambit. Nevertheless, it seems to me that comparison—for the purpose not of judgment but of understanding—is the most direct route to the essence of both *All for Love* and *Antony and Cleopatra.*

> See, see how the Lovers sit in State together,
> As they were giving Laws to half Mankind.
> Th' impression of a smile left in her face,
> Shows she dy'd pleas'd with him for whom she liv'd,
> And went to charm him in another World.
>
> .   .   .   .
>
> Sleep, blest Pair,
> Secure from humane chance, long Ages out,
> While all the storms of Fate fly o'er your Tomb;
> And Fame, to late Posterity, shall tell,
> No lovers liv'd so great, or dy'd so well.[1]

An eerie reversal, as it were, of the last scene of *The Winter's Tale,* the end of *All for Love,* thus presided over and described by the priest Serapion, is a tableau in which the dead lovers turn into statues of themselves, artistically frozen reminders of what, when viewed as a thing of the past, is truly admirable in them, though when it acts as a present reality it must be reprehensible. Dryden has chosen to present his hero's career as past, viewed nostalgically through the failure of both his enterprises at Actium, where love and duty collapse. This is not to say that the decision to begin after the defeat which definitively changes the course of Shakespeare's version denies Dryden the possibility of presenting vivid scenes of amatory and military grandeur. In fact, he finds ways to make both Antony and Cleopatra more unequivocally magnificent, at moments, than Shakespeare generally did in his larger time-scheme. But such moments in *All for Love* are always presented as a self-conscious reenactment of the past, a poignant memory taunting the wretched present.[2] On the whole, critics agree on the essential qualities: as in the earlier heroic plays, rhetoric supplants action; Dryden sentimentalizes the action and the actors;[3] *All for Love* is a characteristically retrospective tragedy in which an "exhausted tragic vision" recalls the dying grandeur of a past now lost.[4]

But one more fact has not been sufficiently stressed: Dryden's protagonists are passive long before they realize themselves fully as a tableau. Because their great decisions are past before the play begins, we see them from the start as acted upon, imprisoned by what has gone before. None of the drive to act, to control, which so marks them in Shakespeare's play is left here. Even the misunderstanding which leads to their deaths arises not from Cleopatra's desperate attempt to reassert her dominance over Antony but as a trick staged by Alexas, just as her pretended flirtation with Dolabella—a much more scrutable phenomenon than her mystifying relationship with Caesar in *Antony and Cleopatra*—is staged by Alexas and by Ventidius, whose language as he arouses Antony's jealousy is a direct imitation of Iago's and thus points clearly to the hero's victimization. With such strategic symmetry Dryden changes the nature of his protagonists and his material.

For all the differences, a good deal of similarity remains between the two plays. Both are about superheroes; both recognize the mythic power of historical personages too large for the constraints of their obligations. Both are problem plays, making their heroes choose constantly and painfully between private and public commitments,[5] between love and duty, and between conflicting desires. In both plays the ultimate commitment to the private entails public destruction in the process of which the lovers' transcendent values are apotheosized.

But against these similarities the fundamental differences are all the more apparent. In *Antony and Cleopatra* the problem belongs as much to the audience as to the protagonists: Shakespeare makes it impossible for anyone who responds fully to feel certain that Antony ought to reject his splendid mistress and share the domination of a mean world with insentient Octavius and imbecile Lepidus, or that he ought to renounce the grandeur of his martial manliness and his obligation to the austere idealism of Rome so that he may trifle away his time in sensual dalliance with a scheming, mercurial, and aging playmate. The power of the play derives in good part from the full and satisfying reality Shakespeare gives to each of the poles between which the hero is drawn, to what I have described elsewhere as the complementarity with which he makes opposed understandings of what life is all about equally and poignantly attractive.[6] If Antony and Cleopatra, driven to the point where no other alternative remains for them, find reconciliation at the last in their desperate deification of one another, the audience is not allowed to take home an unequivocal message that they are right or wrong in doing so: right and wrong are not the answers one is allowed to expect from the Shakespearean tragic universe.

Such is not the case in *All for Love*. Dryden insists that we sympathize with the plight of his protagonists, staging scene after scene in which tears are the appropriate response, but he never for a moment leaves us in doubt as to how to judge the action. Where Shakespeare's opening presents as if by flashes of lightning the opposing valuations of the love affair which will perplex his audience throughout the play, Dryden's offers a different keynote: omens and portents of disaster, a pitying sense of the protagonists' ruin, and a clear understanding that their entanglement, no matter how moving, is a destructive violation of the standards by which right-thinking people have to live. If, prodded to self-defense, Antony can claim that Cleopatra "deserves / More World's than I can lose" (I.368–69), he does so in the full and present knowledge that such commitment unmans him. Consistently both lovers condemn themselves, never denying the operation of standards which they, like everyone else in the play, hold paramount, the hegemony of reason and the sanctity of domestic order. At times in Shakespeare's play Antony's rhetoric of love carries momentary but overwhelming implications of harmony with a cosmos that puts more value in natural process, fecundity, and feeling than it does in social order; but whenever, as at the end of the second act, Dryden's Antony defends his decision to abandon his obligations for Cleopatra, the foolish hyperbole of his rhetoric makes it clear that he is acting against nature. Even in his third-act love duet with Cleopatra his image of the affair is that of Venus and Mars caught out in their adultery by Caesar as a righteous Vulcan: shame is an essential component of his passion. The tension in the characterization of Antony arises not from the struggle between opposite forces within him which the audience is led to recognize as conflicting goods in life itself, but rather from the spectacle of his self-hating entrapment by a passion about which he knows better. Dryden's psychological analysis, expressed in Antony's behavior and Ventidius's succinct description, is shrewd and probing. Its explicitness goes beyond Shakespeare's, for his aim, unlike Shakespeare's, is to provide his audience with a clear understanding of a case which is psychologically complex but morally simple.[7]

That understanding is abetted by Dryden's adroit strategies in other aspects of the play. To have suggested, as Shakespeare had done, that society might not be worth the sacrifices demanded of individuality, would have seriously weakened the assumptions of *All for Love,* and Dryden has ruthlessly eliminated all such hints: Pompey's hypocritical treatment of Menas for offering too explicitly to do the dirty work Pompey would like done; Ventidius's advice to Silius not to achieve too well lest he incur his commander's resentment; Lepidus; Octavius; all allusion to the fickle populace. In order to underline the moral standards, he has unhistorically enlarged the role of Octavia and added her children to the action, so that both Antony and the audience can feel his bond to his family. Perhaps more important, the reflector-character Enobarbus has been subsumed in Ventidius, who retains none of Enobarbus's wavering admiration for both of Antony's worlds. For Ventidius Cleopatra is simply a reprehensible threat to Antony's heroic virtue; he is never the ironist won against his will to share Antony's fascination with her.

Waith suggests that "the moral [of *All for Love*] is not (as Dryden implies) the punishment of lovers who fail to control their passions, but the tragic limitations imposed by human existence on the infinite aspirations of heroic passion."[8] He is right, but the same could be said of *Antony and Cleopatra*. The difference is that by the "human existence" which imposes these limitations Dryden, unlike Shakespeare, means a single, definable entity: a rational universe.[9] In the preface to *All for Love* he asserts that everyone who has previously turned his subject to fiction has been motivated, like him, by "the excellency of the Moral," which he states succinctly: "the chief persons represented, were famous patterns of unlawful love; and their end accordingly was unfortunate" (11.8–10). Because one must judge the lovers harshly, the pity for which the play strives must ultimately be limited:

> That which is wanting to work up the pity to a greater heighth, was not afforded me by the story: for the crimes of love which they both committed, were not occasion'd by any necessity, or fatal ignorance, but were wholly voluntary; since our passions are, or ought to be, within our power. (11.18–21)

This view of passion was many centuries old, of course, and really only a version of what many Renaissance writers had said about the role of reason in the control of one's emotions and the arrangements of one's life. But while the greatest Renaissance writers paid reason the respect de-

Tragic Meanings: The Redactor as Critic

manded by the philosophical and religious traditions they inherited and advanced, they often presented both reason and the emotional life as less simple and comprehensive categories than Dryden's pious assertions make them out to be:

> Let Rome in Tiber melt, and the wide arch
> Of the rang'd empire fall! Here is my space,
> Kingdoms are clay; our dungy earth alike
> Feeds beast as man; the nobleness of life
> Is to do thus [*embracing*]—when such a mutual pair
> And such a twain can do't, in which I bind,
> On pain of punishment, the world to weet
> We stand up peerless.

As Hamlet learns that Polonian scruples are irrelevant to the existential concerns of an inscrutable but inexorable universe, as Lear grows by casting off the accounting methods like those that superficially seem to justify the essential madness of Goneril and Edmund, so Antony begins and ends by appealing to a cosmos that defines human greatness in terms other than those that can be reckoned.

Dryden's view is simpler and clearer. The critical Dolabella agrees with the pitying contempt advocated in the author's preface,[10] but so does Antony in his view that it is "a Fool within me" that takes Cleopatra's part (IV. 562) and his recognition that he has "lost my Reason,...disgrac'd/The name of Soldier with inglorious ease" (I.293–94); and Cleopatra herself uses similar language as she answers Iras's "Call reason to assist you": "I have none./And none would have: my Love's a noble madness....I have lov'd with such transcendent passion,/I soar'd at first, quite out of Reason's view,/And now am lost above it" (II.16–22). Whether they embrace passion or reject it, all Dryden's characters know exactly the rational terms by which others, if not they themselves, can condemn it.

Tragic Meanings: The Redactor as Critic

That so simplistic a definition of reason as a force in human affairs leads almost automatically to precisely the kind of sentimentality about feeling that we find in *All for Love* has been commonplace at least since Eliot named the dissociation of sensibility. Out of the gallimaufry of Renaissance psychology Dryden isolates two principles, clearly opposed, each of which is given a chance to make its claims on us, and we find the opposition between reason and emotion so naive that few of us continue to take his serious drama seriously, despite its frequent psychological acuity and its moral acuity. This is an argument I am tempted to pursue, but it is not the point I am most interested in making here. What differentiates *All for Love* most crucially from *Antony and Cleopatra* is not the contrast between the profundity of Dryden's moral understanding and of Shakespeare's but the sense that the necessary choice, no matter how painful, is clear-cut, that there is a right point of view which the audience shares with the playwright.[11] From that point of view, individualistic and irrational heroism, though sympathetic, can only be judged as misguided. It may be, as Kirsch argues, that the superheroes of Restoration drama are libertines like the rakes of contemporary comedy and the audience's world;[12] but their libertinism is presented in the context of a newly simplistic morality which makes the troublesome moral status of the tragic hero of the Renaissance theater a thing of the past.

Commenting on the demise of the Herculean hero at the end of the seventeenth century, Waith remarks, "The growing sense of civic responsibility which found persuasive advocates in Addison and Steele demanded univocal self-sacrifice of the hero."[13] It is still common for critics of Elizabethan drama to see it in the terms its contemporary defenders employed, as inculcator of civic virtue, sanctuary of the Tudor myth, and the voice of conventional morality—in such terms, that is, as Waith rightly applies to

later drama. Yet looking back at one of the greatest
tragedies of the period from the vantage point of a crucial
theescore years and ten one recognizes Shakespeare's remarkable inability to draw the simple and obvious moral,
the meaning, from a story which, both in its own right and
in its traditional conflation with the myth of Dido and
Aeneas, might reasonably have been expected to turn out
as moralistically in his treatment as in Dryden's.

2

Venice Preserved, unlike *All for Love,* has not earned its place
in history by a professed relationship to Shakespeare, but I
want to argue that it is as self-consciously and as in-
structively modelled on Shakespearean tragedy as Dryden's play. On first consideration, one might guess that
Otway designed his play to produce the kind of ambivalent
response that Shakespeare did. He set out, after all, to
make the tragedy of a political conflict that had polarized
the nation several years earlier, created swings first to the
Whig and then to the Tory side, and, despite its resolution
in favor of the Tories, victims of the abortive "Popish
plot," left neither party wholly untainted.

Furthermore, Otway's strategy appears in a number of
ways to produce problems difficult of resolution. His plot
puts not only the hero but other characters as well in
painful and ultimately inextricable double binds. Since for
most of us the story is not so easy to recall as the crazy
atmosphere, I offer a rudimentary plot summary. The
hero, young Jaffeir, mistreated by his father-in-law, the
Venetian senator Priuli, who has never forgiven him for
marrying Belvidera, is drawn by his close friend Pierre into
a conspiracy fomented by the Spanish ambassador, Be-
damore, and aimed at overthrowing the government. Jaffeir entrusts his beloved wife to the conspirators as a
pledge of his fidelity, along with a dagger which they may

use to kill her should he disappoint them. One of the conspirators, old Renault, takes advantage of the custody to attempt Belvidera's virtue; reporting the outrage to her husband, she turns his loyalty back to the state and exacts his agreement to reveal all to the Senate. Torn between obligations and oaths, Jaffeir gives the list of conspirators to the Senate on condition of pardon for himself and amnesty for his colleagues; but the corrupt senators, led by old Antonio, betray him, and the best the ruined Jaffeir can do is to kill Pierre and himself with the dagger that had once accompanied Belvidera. And she, learning of the demise of her husband and his friend just in time to understand why their bloody ghosts rise on the stage, expires at the end of a mad aria, lamented by her loving father. Clearly the plot is constructed to exploit conflicting loyalties, rival claims.

Otway's characterization reinforces the initial impression of ambivalence. Pierre, linked explicitly with the devil[14] and associated with a gang of vicious conspirators, appears in the early acts as motivated by a neurotic impulse to violence and destruction;[15] when at his arraignment after the conspiracy has been exposed he appeals to the nobility of his cause, the audience must interpret him as a hypocrite; but, by the end, his purity and undying loyalty to his friend and his ideals are facts to which Jaffeir must offer sacrifice. Similarly Priuli, who begins the play as a heavy father causelessly cruel to the young man who has not only married his daughter but earlier saved her life, is given a fifth-act soliloquy in which we are led to believe that he is a loving and suffering father motivated by grief over her marriage to a man who has now confirmed Priuli's initial fears by betraying both her and the state. And the contrast between the high-flying idealism of both senatorial and conspiratorial rhetoric and the ugly self-interestedness of political activity in both camps seems like further evidence of an ambivalent structure.

Tragic Meanings: The Redactor as Critic

Otway complicates his political presentation by constructing symmetrical betrayals on each side: Belvidera is
betrayed by the conspirators, the conspirators by the Senate. More notable than this, however, is his treatment of
Shaftesbury, the historical villain he mocks. Otway vigor-
ously sought out court patronage; he dedicated the play,
with a profusion of Tory sentiments, to Charles II's mistress; and he wrote a special epilogue for a performance
favored by the Duke of York himself, the target of
Shaftesbury's plot. In view of all this it is surprising to
discover that Otway split Shaftesbury into *two* characters,
lecherous old villains motivated politically only by lust and
whim who play parallel roles on opposite sides: Antonio
among the senators degrades Pierre's mistress Aquilina
and drives her lover into rebellion; Renault among the
conspirators attempts to violate Belvidera and motivates
her husband to abandon the conspiracy. Otway calls attention to the obvious parallel by using the same verbal tag to
characterize both old men.[16] This is a familiar Elizabethan
device, of course, and others seem to serve the same purpose of establishing a thematically complicating symmetry.[17]

But more than anything else that tempts one to look for
Elizabethan complexity in *Venice Preserved* is the ostentatious modelling on Shakespearean tragedy. Priuli addresses
the Senate virtually in the words of Richard II lamenting
his fate;[18] Jaffeir curses like Lear and Timon;[19] Belvidera
begins a speech in that vein only to end it like Macbeth;[20]
a walking anthology, she concludes the play and her life in
a mad scene that unmistakably recalls Ophelia. If the play
thus closes with memories of *Hamlet,* it opens with signals
that the Venetian tragedy may be a version of *Othello.*
Brabantio-like, Priuli accuses Jaffeir of having wronged
him by taking advantage of the kindnesses the Senator had
done him upon the young man's return from travel and of
having stolen his daughter at dead of night.[21] Though Jaf-

feir has done more than tell stories of his adventures, in fact has rescued the daughter from accidental drowning, his defense echoes the famous simplicity of Othello's.[22]

But all these allusions are misleading: the significant model for *Venice Preserved* is *Julius Caesar*. The first act replays the temptation episode of Shakespeare's political tragedy as Pierre plays Cassius to Jaffeir's Brutus, shrewdly working on his disaffection, his concern for "the public good" (I.208), his political idealism, and his patriotism, and heating Jaffeir's emotions with lurid accounts of Priuli's villainy in order to lure him into a conspiracy already under way. The temptation succeeds in a nocturnal meeting on the streets as the clock strikes, which recalls similar meetings in *Julius Caesar* and leads to an indoor scene among conspirators who, like Shakespeare's, comment on the passing of darkness and the approach of dawn, welcome Jaffeir into their company, establish their code, and plan for the overthrow of the government. Explicit comparisons are repeatedly made to the assassination of Caesar; Jaffeir sees the conspirators as too noble to need oaths; Pierre is likened to Cassius (II.iii.59); and when Belvidera joins Jaffeir, they self-consciously reenact the roles of Portia and Brutus.[23] Unlike the allusions to other plays, the ones to *Julius Caesar* are not adventitious: Cassius provides a key to the combination of patriotic rhetoric and conspiratorial predilection in Pierre; more importantly Belvidera like Portia focuses for her husband the cruel conflict between loyalties that his situation has aroused. Otway is a skillful dramatist dealing with a political situation which by his time he must have known to be more complicated than the view taken of it by any of its participants, and he has chosen to base his portrayal of the events on the tragedy in which Shakespeare perhaps most sharply explores the contradictions that so mock attempts to redeem history through decisive action, the insight and self-deception, idealism and vanity, public and private

interest so inseparably intertwined in the character of op-
pressors and oppressed as both to demand and to vitiate
decisive action.

But the real lessons of Shakespearean tragedy were lost
on Otway, for despite its model *Venice Preserved* lacks the
complex understanding of the world that dictates and
justifies Shakespeare's handling of his materials. In the first
place, ignoring the issues on which the English events that
provoked the play turned and the difficulties in Venice
that enabled the historical Bedamar to raise his conspiracy,[24] Otway has constructed a political tragedy without politics. The conspirators have no ideological justification. The wicked Renault makes it clear that he longs to
take advantage of Venice in its adversity, to kill, burn,
terrorize mercilessly, and "possess / That seat of empire
which our souls were framed for" (II.iii.82–83); Be-
damore, in the service of Spain, proposes to make "Venice
own us for her lords" (II.iii.195). So much for liberty.
Only Jaffeir and Pierre talk of lofty ideals, and both of
them are curiously ready to burn the city down to save it.[25]
They talk of liberty, vile oppression, and the betrayal of
justice, but their protests move characteristically from
total abstraction to the personal outrages they have suffered in their sexual lives. As for the senators, their betrayal of Jaffeir only confirms their hypocrisy. Their representative type is the extraordinary old Antonio, pursuing
his mistress Aquilina through the play's most notorious
scenes in a horrifying stream of baby talk, acting out the
fantasy that he is a dog, and begging his mistress to spit on
him.[26] The play assumes that there are no real issues in
politics and that the same kind of hypocrisy obtains on
both sides of the contention; certainly it poses no political
problem for the audience, which is given little to admire in
either faction.

The depoliticization of political materials is most sig-
nally revealed by the substitution of sex for other prob-

Tragic Meanings: The Redactor as Critic

lems. If the moving concerns of Pierre and Jaffeir are the fates of two young women, the crucial offenses of the villains on both sides are correspondingly sexual. Renault's lust not only undoes the conspirators but also serves as the index of their iniquity; Antonio's pathological relationship with Aquilina and Priuli's rejection of his son-in-law constitute virtually all that one can hold against the senators until they betray Jaffeir. Though Otway wants us to think of Shakespeare, the great model for his sexualizing and defusing of political issues is rather Beaumont and Fletcher; and his play resembles theirs in other ways. Like the Fletcherian plays Waith has definitively described,[27] *Venice Preserved* so romanticizes a real historical setting as to lose any historical credibility: Venice is a fantasy world with a real name. As in Beaumont and Fletcher the plot is based on an improbable hypothesis, Jaffeir's having given the conspirators his wife—his sole concern in life—as a pledge and then finding himself obligated, by their mistreatment of her and by her own imploring, to betray them and risk her life. Significantly, the whole Belvidera business, the mainspring of the play, is Otway's invention. And the impossible puzzle is solved luridly enough to have pleased Fletcher himself: the dagger with which Jaffeir has authorized the conspirators to kill Belvidera, should he betray them, ends up in his hands, and in a scene of homosexual ardor he uses it to kill not Belvidera but Pierre and himself; Belvidera, left to fend for herself, expires unaided only, apparently, because the play has reached its end. The protean characterization already mentioned is similarly Fletcherian, serving startling effect rather than consistency. Jaffeir's movement from Belvidera to Pierre recalls Amintor in *The Maid's Tragedy*, and interestingly enough his situation at any point in *Venice Preserved* involves, like that of the Fletcherian hero, an excruciating need to choose between opposed goods: loyalty to his wife and rebellion for her sake against her beloved father; revenge for her wrongs against the fact that such revenge will destroy her; obligations to both the state and the conspiracy. And as in Beaumont and Fletcher the focus of a play peopled by conflict-ridden characters is on abnormal psychology presented through high-flown rhetoric.

Venice Preserved is not an ineffective play. It sacrifices one kind of power in order to achieve another, as can perhaps be seen most clearly if one looks again to see what use Otway makes of his Shakespearean material. Consider, for instance, the curses intoned by Jaffeir and Belvidera. What makes their precedents so shaking in *King Lear* is the degree to which the audience, regardless of its awareness of Lear's inability to come to terms with his own complicity in his misery, is forced to feel as its own the longing for annihilation that has overcome him, to entertain painfully the suspicion that in his hatred of all that brings such wretched life into being he may be essentially right. But the plot of *Venice Preserved* gives no such resonance to the curses of Jaffeir and Belvidera, who are pitifully trapped by a set of circumstances so odd, and so unrelated to any kind of cosmic force that could be suggested by the dramatization, as to make them objects of detached wonder and sentimental pity rather than types of the human condition caught in the nature of things. Jaffeir's predicament, to be sure, can be described in terms of a characteristic human dilemma, the necessity to choose between wife and friend, between the desire for revenge (dressed up as a fight for liberty) and a conservative fear of disorder. Unlike such dilemmas in Shakespeare, however, Jaffeir's is not only schematically neat and problematic, but also luridly operatic; one is as likely to be titillated by its exotic uniqueness as convinced of its relevance to one's own human possibilities.

Perhaps because Otway puts more energy into the analogies with *Julius Caesar,* his distance from its essential

quality is more revealing. The initial encounters between
Jaffeir and Pierre recall *Julius Caesar,* to be sure. But we
remember a Brutus motivated by a melancholy whose
source he cannot sound and by a combination of patriotism, idealism, and egotism; a Cassius moved by the
restlessness so shrewdly diagnosed by Caesar himself and
by an almost pathological inability to live in the shade of
nominal superiors who have proved themselves all too
mortal. The motives of these characters are ultimately as
complex as they are. Like their historical counterparts,
Brutus and Cassius are beyond simple moral or psychological formulation, and disagreement properly continues
to rage about Shakespeare's characters as about their
originals and about the real meaning and value of their
conspiracy. Shakespeare bases his tragedy on the opacity
of history: did Caesar really plan to end the republic and
become king? If so, what was the proper course of action
for a republican Roman? Can any action be free from
self-interest? If not, should one not act? Is reason the
proper—or a possible—basis for political action? If not,
what is? But Otway deftly removes from his model all
incitement to such questions: there is no mysterious Julius
Caesar at the center of things, and if *Venice Preserved* shows
the principal conspirators to have mixed motives, it does
so in order to make us disapprove or sympathize. Jaffeir
and Pierre travesty their prototypes, the former driven
merely by chagrin over Priuli's mistreatment of Belvidera,
which he sees as a political matter; the latter moved by
Aquilina's subjection to Antonio, which allows him to play
out a diabolical nihilism more obviously dominant and
more contemptible than Cassius's drive. Since Aquilina
has voluntarily sold her charms to Antonio, the legitimacy
of Pierre's anger cannot be Otway's point; the play is more
concerned with establishing Pierre as the instrument
through which a thoroughly evil conspiracy seduces the
innocent Jaffeir. And though Jaffeir's concern for his poor

wife is touching, it is as she herself makes clear the wrong basis for an idealistic decision to join the enemies of Venice.

Accordingly, the analogy to the Roman conspiracy is promptly qualified by Pierre's appeal to Catiline's indefensible plot as a model; and even though in fact Venetian authority is presented as far more corrupt and dangerous than Caesar's, which Brutus himself admitted was only potentially evil, the reaction against it is painted as still more despicable. If Brutus is misguided but high-minded in his attempt to make a holy band of his colleagues and a sacred ritual of a murder, Jaffeir's adulation of his vicious cronies is patently stupid,[28] and his desire to see the rebellion as political is constantly undercut by its sexual basis. In this light we may consider the role of Belvidera as Portia. Brutus's stoic wife reinforces the ambiguity of his predicament: daughter of one of the saints of the Roman republic, she embodies the values for which her husband strikes Caesar down; carefully excluded from the conspiracy, she is an implicit critic of the self-defining criminality of the assassination; left by Brutus to her lonely and orthodox suicide, she is the final indication that the conspiracy has failed both morally and politically; as a memory, she remains an index of the virtues that Brutus fleetingly embodies and his successors lack; and her death provides the fulcrum of the great quarrel and reconciliation between Brutus and Cassius. In short, she is an essential part of the intricate design of a play which demands conflicting responses of its audience. Otway recognized Portia's ambiguity but translated it into a battle of values which only the protagonist, not the audience, can experience: as victim of Priuli she sparks Jaffeir's decision to kill her father; as victim of Renault, she spurs Jaffeir's return to Priuli's camp; as moral spokesman she is unwaveringly the enemy of the conspiracy and the voice of loyalist sentiment.[29]

Tragic Meanings: The Redactor as Critic

In *Julius Caesar* the protagonist embodies our highest hopes and worst fears about ourselves: the best man in the play's world, he is driven at least in part by what is best in himself to what turns out to be the worst possible thing he could have done, and his fate makes us recognize the play's world as that of Shakespearean tragedy. But in *Venice Preserved* there is no problem for us, and the hero is cast in a different light: watching him from a position of superior moral knowledge, we see him as passive, foolishly ambivalent, incapable of significant action, and hysterical in rhetoric as in deeds; a needless troublemaker; a simple warning not to act on the basis of passion. His message is that heroism is not, as in Shakespeare, the fullest acting out of human potentiality, but a spectacular deviation from the norm, wonderful in its size and scope and reassuring in its irrelevance to the concerns of real life. Otway has moved the arena of ambivalence from the audience's psyche to the hero's. Though Jaffeir is more frequently and outspokenly aware of his conflicting obligations than Brutus, we are encouraged to watch his agony without finding ourselves on both sides of his problem. In so changing the nature of tragedy, Otway has repeated the change brought about by the Restoration stage itself: we look at an action in which we are no longer forced to be participants.

3

If what I have claimed is true about two free and imaginative improvisations on the model of Shakespearean tragedy, it is more startlingly so about the period's direct adaptations of the tragedies themselves. Shakespeare fascinated Restoration audiences but apparently could not be taken straight.[30] The radical modifications made by his adapters consist not so much of the neoclassical regularization one might expect as of attempts to focus the problematic qualities of the tragedies, to tame them and make them vehicles for providing comfort and reassurance and lucid understanding to their audiences. By examining the most significant changes in the five most famous tragic adaptations of the quarter-century between 1674 and 1700, we may learn a great deal about the Restoration period, perhaps even more about Shakespeare.

The most notorious and successful is Nahum Tate's *The History of King Lear*,[31] which generations found more bearable than its original. And for good reason. At the end of Tate's play, with Lear and Gloucester snatched from the horrors they have lived through and reunited with the virtuous members of their families, a triumphant Edgar mounts the throne as husband to Cordelia. His last words epitomize the play:

> Thy bright Example shall convince the World
> (Whatever Storms of Fortune are decreed)
> That Truth and Vertue shall at last succeed.

These words only confirm what Cordelia has said, on hearing of the happy resolution of all problems, in words that seem designed to confute Shakespeare, "Then there are Gods, and Vertue is their Care" (V.vi.97). The questions raised every time such a sentiment is ventured in Shakespeare's *Lear* measure the difference between the two plays, and every decision Tate has made emphasizes his intention to clear up all the ambiguities of the tragedy. Edmund, Goneril, and Regan are stripped of that peculiar blend of logicality and keen perceptiveness which papers over the horror of their real motivations, and Edmund is converted to a stage tyrant, yearning to rule cruelly and absolutely; thus the play's evil is conventionalized, motivated, isolated. Tate rationalizes the odd behavior of the principal virtuous characters by the deft expedient of the love affair, which as he argues in his preface gives probability to both Cordelia's silence and the otherwise almost inexplicable cruelty contingent on Edgar's disguise. Cordelia dare not speak her love for her father lest he give her so big a dowry that she will be irresistible to Burgundy, Lear's choice, when it is Edgar she wants to marry; Lear's anger is no more than the conventional outrage of the comic heavy father thwarted by his daughter's romance, and it leads naturally to his reformation and his forgiveness of her fifth-act marriage. And there is no more mystery about Edgar, whose gratuitously wounding behavior has puzzled some of the best recent critics of Shakespeare's play:[32] in a scene contiguous and parallel to the one in which Kent makes himself Lear's servant, Edgar assumes his disguise in order to help Cordelia. Even Gloucester's plan to hurl himself off Dover Cliff is explained as a stratagem to arouse sympathy for Lear.

Simply to describe Tate's reduction of *King Lear* to this uncomplicated comic contest is enough to recall the terrifying convolutions and perplexities of Shakespeare's tragedy, in which we are not permitted to resolve the conflicts between views of the cosmos as savage, benign, retributive, indifferent, rational, or bestial, or to understand any character according to any single principle. No extended critical analysis is required here to demonstrate how far beyond successful reduction Shakespeare's tragedy lies; that has been the point of every successful recent critical study of *King Lear*.[33] Nahum Tate, in his recognition and elimination of everything that makes *Lear* genuinely Shakespearean and genuinely tragic, is nothing less than brilliant.

4

If Tate gives *King Lear* a simple meaning by making it a comedy, Cibber and Davenant do the same, respectively, for *Richard III* and *Macbeth* by making them more conventional tragedies. The problem posed by these two plays, of course, is that their heroes would serve admirably as villains of almost any other play, and this is precisely what comes of them in revision. The peculiarity of Shake-

Tragic Meanings: The Redactor as Critic

speare's achievements grows strikingly apparent when they are compared to their Restoration versions.

Richard III deserves extended study in the present context. It is the first of Shakespeare's great plays. It virtually leaps to its eminence out of its context as the climax of the daringly conceived York tetralogy, ending the recurrent search for a genre that flickers through the earlier plays by turning at the last into the play in which Shakespeare discovers tragedy. Like the Marlovian ambiance from which it emerges, like *Titus Andronicus,* it is a villain tragedy, and as in the greater plays with which it can be compared it is a tragedy, not a moralistic celebration of the retribution the hero brings down on his own head, because the evil by which the protagonist operates is in some sense his own tragedy, his daimon, his nemesis, the inscrutable source of his energy and his destruction. Shakespeare's Richard is both terrifying and like later tragic heroes—Macbeth in particular—because he is motivated not by the ambition of a Claudius or of his own materialistic father, but by a self-destructive and mysterious yearning which drives him to his glory and his death. What Richard does not understand about himself, and Shakespeare permits us to see, is that the true center of his motivation is his hatred for his family and ultimately for himself. Looking at the *Henry VI* plays, one is tempted to believe that Shakespeare stumbled into this perception: having hit on the idea of organizing the inchoate materials for his gigantic tetralogy around the central figure of the family, he discovered in *Richard III* that that figure had entirely other implications than what he had previously dramatized. In the *Henry VI* plays, to put it bluntly, he begins intellectually, like a bright young playwright, with a concept of the family as the cause of problems in a society governed by primogeniture and of the family as model of both social integration and social breakdown; but he moves at the end to a perception—not to a concept, be it noted—of the family, internalized, as the mysterious and worrisome source of the most destructive human behavior. We shall come to our fullest understanding of what Shakespeare discovered in composing *Richard III* by looking at what Colley Cibber did to the play, but in order to be sure of that understanding we must watch the development of the tragedy in its context.

5

The basic motif of *Henry VI, Part One,* is the overthrow of the old family structure of a paradisal England. In the royal family this is represented by the opening dead march for Henry V, strong father of a weak son; by the young King's inability to rule decisively;[34] and by Suffolk's final scheme to rule the King and realm through an adulterous affair with the new Queen.

More generally, England's problems, like those of France, are repeatedly imaged in terms of unhappy families. Lamenting at the funeral of Henry V that arms no longer avail, Bedford bids posterity

> await for wretched years,
> When at their mothers' moist'ned eyes babes shall suck,
> Our isle be made a nourish of salt tears,
> And none but women left to wail the dead. (I.i.48–51)

Within two scenes the outrageous Winchester accuses Gloucester of playing Cain to his Abel (I.iii.39), and their tedious conflict is couched throughout in the language of intrafamilial flyting: "thou bastard of my grandfather," Gloucester calls Winchester (III.1.42), and his loyal servant, who sees him as "so kind a father of the commonweal," pledges that "We and our wives and children all will fight" for him (II.i.98–100). Significantly, the issue of this crucial scene in the middle of the play is blood and inheritance, and here the inept King unnecessarily makes up for Richard Plantagenet's lost inheritance (improperly forfeited when Henry V executed Richard's father as a traitor without first trying him), by making him Duke of York:

> But all the whole inheritance I give
> That doth belong unto the house of York,
> From whence you spring by lineal descent.
> (III.i.163–65)

In the Temple Garden scene and throughout, the family serves as model for England's troubles not only because the dissension is in fact within the extended royal family, but more importantly because like the body the family is the traditional image of organic wholeness:

> As fest'red members rot but by degree,
> Till bones and flesh and sinews fall away,
> So will this base and envious discord breed.
> (III.i.191–93)[35]

The contrasting positive image of familial harmony is presented, ironically, as the Yorkists gather round the dying Mortimer. In the presence of the moribund patriarch, the constant use of endearing apostrophes to fathers, uncles, nephews, and the like sets off the more modern squabbling we have witnessed (II.v).

But two characters I have not mentioned, the most famous figures in the play, point more forcefully to the central metaphor of family. Set against one another in respect of class, sex, national allegiance, character, and even the historical movements and periods they represent, Lord Talbot and Joan of Arc, the Pucelle, play out their conflicting ideals in symmetrical acts of familial commitment. In a world exemplified by the coming apart of families, Talbot's loyalty to his own—his name, or its past, and his son, or its future—is as anachronistic as the chivalric ideals of a sword-fighter in a day when a scarcely fledged gunner's son can shoot down a hero as well as his own father with the unchivalric weapons that ended the Hundred Years'

Tragic Meanings: The Redactor as Critic

War (I.iv). At every point, Talbot's chivalric code is patriarchal, appropriate to the idea of the family that characterized the feudal period and that Lawrence Stone sees as dying in Shakespeare's own day.[36] In his funeral oration for the swordsman cut down by French fire Talbot evinces appropriate veneration for the continuation of the social order by promising to build a public monument to Salisbury (II.ii). In an episode that begins in the very same scene, as the Countess of Auvergne tries to entrap Talbot at a private entertainment, Talbot riddlingly says he is only the shadow of himself, then shows what he means by demonstrating his true substance as the concealed troops waiting to save him:

> You are deceiv'd, my substance is not here;
> For what you see is but the smallest part
> And least proportion of humanity.
> I tell you, madam, were the whole frame here,
> It is of such a spacious lofty pitch,
> Your roof were not sufficient to contain't.

> (II.iii.50–56)

As Edward Berry observes, Talbot identifies himself literally with the entire chivalric community, presenting an image of social wholeness in which the individual alone is only a fragment and making a vivid contrast to the future Richard III, who will proclaim at the end of 3 Henry VI, "I am myself alone."[37] To such a patriarchal hero as Talbot, Joan's reversal of sexual roles—"A woman clad in armor chaseth" the English troops, he exclaims bitterly (I.v.3)—is as presumptuous as her false claim to be descended from "a gentler blood" (V.iv.8).

Talbot's most famous moment is the last battle of the Hundred Years' War, in which, in a Virgilian scene, the old man watches his son die before him: "Now my old arms are young John Talbot's grave" (IV.vii.32). David Riggs has argued persuasively that this episode represents the last stand of English chivalry as well as the end of a particular aristocratic line.[38] Before the end, Talbot urges his son to leave him on the battlefield, and the boy's dilemma is posed entirely in family terms. If he stays, he will be killed and his family will die; but if he leaves to save himself, the family name will die. The debate is conducted in the rhetoric of tragedy:

> TAL. Shall all thy mother's hopes lie in one tomb?
> JOHN. Ay, rather than I'll shame my mother's womb.
> (IV.v.34–35)

> TAL. Part of thy father may be sav'd in thee.
> JOHN. No part of him but will be shame in me.
> (IV.v.38–39)

> JOHN. For live I will not if my father die.
> TAL. Then here I take my leave of thee, fair son,
> Born to eclipse thy life this afternoon.
> Come, side by side, together live and die,
> And soul with soul from France to heaven fly.
> (IV.v.51–55)

Calling the Dolphin a bastard, Talbot urges his son to fly, but the young man prefers to die at his father's feet. Talbot, he argues, is twice his father, and he twice his father's son since the old man has saved the younger and given him life again; Talbot, acceding to his son's desire to fight alongside of him even to the death, sees him as Icarus. Designed as the emotional climax of the play, this episode is the defining moment, an emblem of the family as the matrix of history.

Against that emblem is set the deracinated Joan of Arc. Her boast that she exceeds her sex (I.ii.90) is another version of the threat that this mock-Tamburlaine, a shepherd's daughter risen to military command, poses to the aristocratic ideals of military service and gentle blood, whose formalities she ridicules as nothing more than a "silly-stately style" (V.i.72).[39] If in her anti-aristocratic stance she threatens the stability of Talbot's class, so in her parody of the courtly mistress as she plays inamorata to the debile Dolphin does she subvert the romantic code of chivalric heroism (I.ii.107–20). But her deepest opposition to Talbot is in her contempt for family. So little is she concerned with name, in the sense meant by Talbot's son, that she denies the legitimacy of her own birth in order to claim her social superiority, simultaneously striking at the bond of familial love and destroying her own honor:

> Decrepit miser! base ignoble wretch!
> I am descended of a gentler blood.
> Thou art no father nor no friend of mine. (V.iv.7–9)

> SHEP. Kneel down and take my blessing, good my
> girl.
> Wilt thou not stoop? Now cursed be the time
> Of thy nativity. (V.iv.25–27)

> PUC. Not me begotten of a shepherd swain,
> But issued from the progeny of kings. (V.iv.37–38)

It is both in character and appropriate to the familial ideal that ironically underlies the chaos of *1 Henry VI* that Joan should claim at the outset that Christ's mother supports her (I.ii.106) and at the end, after pleading for her life on the grounds that she is a virgin, that she is about to bear an illegitimate child.

The second play in the cycle widens the topsy-turviness introduced in *Part One*. Grown to feeble manhood and no longer protected by the staff which his father had given Humphrey Duke of Gloucester, the King is undermined by rebellious subjects, from the rabble led by Jack Cade up to the Duke of York and the treacherous Queen. At the heart of England's troubles is the dynastic quarrel rehearsed in full detail from the Yorkist point of view (II.ii). But once again family is not so much the cause as the paradigm of the problem. The play opens with the reading of a marriage contract between the King and Margaret of Anjou, a mistake on every count, since, as Gloucester points out immediately, the price in French territory that England must pay is excessive; since, as events prove, Margaret, ruling her weak husband through deception and brassy nerve, reverses sexual roles as much as Joan of Arc did in *Part One*; and since the Queen's betrayal of her husband's royal prerogatives originates in an adulterous betrayal of their marriage itself. The Duke of York, aspirant to Henry's crown, is motivated not by the patriarchal patriotism implicit in his dynastic claims but by a consistently commercial interest in the value of the crown and its real estate. At the end, he and his murderous sons form a parodistic image of the ideal family, especially set as they are against the ideal image presented by the Cliffords father and son: the loyal old man killed in defense of his king and carried off the battlefield on the back of his young son, who recognizes the ironic comparison between the stage emblem they present and the familiar image of Aeneas walking into the future with his live father on his back. If the Cliffords recall the Talbots of *Part One,* the central dramatic episode of *Part Two* presents a new familial device as image of England's breakdown: the Duke of Gloucester forced by his anachronistic sense of justice to abandon his treacherous Duchess as, caught in her scheme, she is carried off to punishment. Here again, as in the action of King and Queen, an aggressive and ambitious wife plots to thwart her husband's patriotic concerns. The center cannot hold.

Henry VI, Part Three opens with the line, "I wonder how the King escap'd our hands" and closes with the killing of the King. The civil violence confined in the earlier parts to lower victims now climactically assaults the national patriarchy itself. Appropriately, the vehicle for the play's multi-

ple regicide is the revenge tragedy, with its ceaseless
dialectic of blood and its basis in the torn family. As dex-
terously as in *Titus Andronicus,* Shakespeare outdoes the
conventional plot by setting *two* bloody families against
one another. On the one side we meet the monstrous
York clan in a typical moment of show and tell:

> EDW. Lord Stafford's father, Duke of Buckingham,
> Is either slain or wounded dangerous;
> I cleft his beaver with a downright blow.
> That this is true, father, behold his blood.
>   MON[TAGUE]. And, brother, here's the Earl of
>   Wiltshire's blood,
> Whom I encount'red as the battles join'd.
>   RICH. Speak thou for me and tell them what I did.
>   [*Showing the Duke of Somerset's head.*]
>   YORK. Richard hath best deserv'd of all my sons.
>   (I.i.10–17)

On the other we meet the equally charming Lancastrians:

> Plantagenet, of thee and these thy sons,
> Thy kinsmen and thy friends, I'll have more lives
> Than drops of blood were in my father's veins.
>   (I.i.95–97)

As the play opens the two family branches bicker over the
legality of various heirs to the kingdom; hoping vainly to
end the quarrel, the King adopts the Duke of York as his
son and heir, thus wronging his own son the Prince of
Wales despite the latter's protestations against such un-
natural behavior.

The revenge ethic and its theatrical dynamic dominate
the play. Thus Clifford turns villain in avenging the death
of his father against the Earl of Rutland, the young son of
Old Clifford's murderer.

> EDW. And now the battle's ended,
> If friend or foe, let him be gently used.

RICH. Revoke that doom of mercy, for 'tis Clifford,
Who, not contented that he lopp'd the branch
In hewing Rutland when his leaves put forth,
But set his murth'ring knife unto the root
From whence that tender spray did sweetly spring,
I mean our princely father, Duke of York.
WAR. From off the gates of York fetch down the head,
Your father's head, which Clifford placed there;
In stead whereof let this supply the room:
Measure for measure must be answered.   (II.vi.43–55)

Central though it is, however, the revenge idea of the
family is not the only image of kinship at work in the play.
"*Alarum. Enter a SON that hath kill'd his father, at one door,
[dragging the dead body] . . . . Enter [a] FATHER that hath
kill'd his son, at another door, bearing of his son*" (II.v.53SD,
78SD). With this famous emblem Shakespeare employs a
heavy-handed symmetry he will soon abandon to symbolize
the kinslaughtering dissension that is destroying England.

SON. Was ever son so ru'd a father's death?
FATH. Was ever father so bemoan'd his son?
(II.v.109–10)

But the York family itself provides a new image of the
family, which will be the controlling idea of *Richard
III*—the family as an unstable grouping of autonomous
individualists each operating for himself. Richard Plantagenet's impulsive eldest son is a fine example. Having
succeeded his father as head of family and, through the
deposition of Henry VI, become king for a day, Edward
foolishly marries Lady Grey, shattering the necessary
dynastic arrangements for which Warwick the Kingmaker
has gone to France and, in Clarence's words, leaving "your
brothers to go speed elsewhere"; as Richard charges, "in
your bride you bury brotherhood" (IV.i.58, 55). Edward's
selfish action gives Richard the opportunity he requires to

begin constructing his murderous masterpiece, and at the moment at which the York line has at last put a member on the throne—even before King Edward kills his cousin Henry VI himself—the family begins to fall victim to the savagery of its best-remembered scion, Richard, Duke of Gloucester. Standing together as they murder the Lancastrian royal family, the York boys themselves constitute a hideous parody of the family.

Shakespeare does not let his audience miss the point. For back at the center of the play he has given Richard the famous soliloquy (III.ii.124–95) in which the hunchback uses his deformity—his mother's curse on him, as he sees it—to justify the murder of his own family.

> Ay, Edward will use women honorably.
> Would he were wasted, marrow, bones, and all,
> That from his loins no hopeful branch may spring,
> To cross me from the golden time I look for!
> And yet, between my soul's desire and me—
> The lustful Edward's title buried—
> Is Clarence, Henry, and his young son Edward,
> And all the unlook'd for issue of their bodies
> To take their rooms, ere I can place myself:
> A cold premeditation for my purpose! (124–33)

Against one last ideal familial image, the benign patriarchy of the now young Earl of Richmond forecast by old Henry VI, stands the fratricidal Richard, his crimes against his family justified in his mind by the fact that "love forswore me in my mother's womb" (III.ii.153), his ability to kill a kinsman without "pity, love, nor fear" (V.vi.68) excused because he was born legs first. The climactic horror of a cycle that has presented England's civil broils as the strife of a ruined family is a monster who is licensed to do anything he wants because, like Wagner's Alberich renouncing love, he can deny his own family bond, in words that will come back to haunt him at the end of *Richard III:*

> I have no brother, I am like no brother;
> And this word "love," which greybeards call divine,
> Be resident in men like one another,
> And not in me: I am myself alone.   (V.vi.80–83)

6

The three Henry VI plays have presented England's crisis not primarily as a struggle between Marlovian entrepreneurs greedy for power but as the anguish of a family gone sour. It is certainly significant, therefore, that as a supreme villain emerges from chaos he is presented as motivated not by dreams of glory but by a nihilistic and universal hatred. *Der Geist der stets verneint,* Richard internalizes the fratricidal struggle that generations of his clan have acted out. As Shakespeare makes us perceive this essential quality of Richard's character, he makes us understand that the family has become something other than what it was earlier in the cycle: no longer simply the paradigm but actually the cause of historical events. As he will do so often in his later career, Shakespeare tempts us to try out other explanations for a character's behavior and forces us to reject them. Thus in the opening soliloquy of *Richard III* the hunchback King once again offers us an argument that his misbehavior results from his physical deformity, an argument which Freud accepted at face value but which, as Clemen suggests, an Elizabethan audience would have been less likely to credit.[40] Richard's complaint that he is "not shap'd for sportive tricks" (I.i.15) and cannot appeal to women, followed almost immediately by his self-confident and triumphant wooing of the woman least likely to succumb to his advances, suggests that he does not believe his own analysis.

The greater temptation for us as for Shakespeare's first audience must be to see Richard as a Tamburlainian over-reacher like Joan of Arc, for whom kinsmen are simply steps to the throne.

> Whiles I in Ireland nourish a mighty band,
> I will stir up in England some black storm
> Shall blow ten thousand souls to heaven or hell;
> And this fell tempest shall not cease to rage
> Until the golden circuit on my head,
> Like to the glorious sun's transparent beams,
> Do calm the fury of this mad-bred flaw. (2 *Henry VI,*
> III.1.348–54)

Such lines, drunk with the glory of that golden circuit, are indeed what one might expect of Richard. But in fact he does not speak them: these are the words of his more conventionally ambitious father—just as it is the aspiring Lady Macbeth, not her hagridden husband, who fantasizes "the golden round" (*Macbeth,* I.v.28). Only once does Richard sound the true Tamburlainian note:

> How sweet a thing it is to wear a crown,
> Within whose circuit is Elysium
> And all that poets feign of bliss and joy. (3 *Henry VI,*
> I.ii.29–31)

And these words are mere Ricardian rhetoric, designed to perk up the flagging spirits of his father, whom they persuade to "be king, or die." For Richard himself, as for Cressida, "Joy's soul lies in the doing" (*Tr.,* I.ii.287). We perceive him, as ultimately do all about him, as diabolical—that is, as inexplicably and gratuitously evil—precisely because he is motivated not by the prize at the end but by the journey itself. His self-psychologizing is as disingenuous and shallow as Iago's self-searching, and we must judge his behavior not by his explanations but by what we see. Richard kills his family not because he wants to be king but because he wants to kill his family.[41]

The primary evidence is the structure of *Richard III,* which imitates the parabola of its protagonist's inner life. Just as in *Macbeth,* we watch the hero move as in a nightmare, without a moment's pause to enjoy the fruits of his conquest, from a course of Machiavellian scheming and ruthless slaughter to a denouement of terror and psychological breakdown.

After all his work, Richard spends precisely one and one-half lines of blank verse celebrating his victory before he acknowledges what he has not allowed himself to think before: that he has entrapped himself, that after such a rise there is only the impossibility of holding and enjoying power.

> [*Here he ascendeth the throne.*] *Sound.*
> Thus high, by thy advice
> And thy assistance, is King Richard seated;
> But shall we wear these glories for a day?
> Or shall they last, and we rejoice in them?
> (IV.ii.3–6)

It is here, at the very moment of his coronation, that Richard must plan the worst of his crimes, the murder of the children in the Tower; here, at the height of his rise, for the first time he must speak in asides that reflect not sardonic pleasure but terror in his heart:

> I must be married to my brother's daughter,
> Or else my kingdom stands on brittle glass.
> Murther her brothers and then marry her—
> Uncertain way of gain! But I am in
> So far in blood that sin will pluck on sin,
> Tear-falling pity dwells not in this eye. (IV.ii.60–65)

What before filled him with the joy of doing he now recognizes as a pointless compulsion; he knows now that he acts not to reach a static condition of glorious power but to continue a pattern he has locked himself into, in which everyone around him must become his victim until he himself, rejected even by his mother and utterly alone, is destroyed: "Alack, I love myself," he will lament, unable to commit the revenge against himself that he learns, in the dark night of his soul, is all that is left to him:

> Alack, I love myself. Wherefore? For any good
> That I myself have done unto myself?
> O no! Alas, I rather hate myself
> For hateful deeds committed by myself.
> I am a villain; yet I lie, I am not.   (V.iii.187–91)

For a final moment, with a gusto that makes his nemesis Richmond sound like a perfunctory bureaucrat, he can still urge his troops to a battle that must end in disaster, but even in this ironically redemptive moment Richard's true and only pleasure is the deed itself. That pleasure, of course, makes Richard a black comic masterpiece, a surrogate playwright, a saturnalian actor-out of universal human aggressiveness, a vice-presenter whose hideous and joyous triumphs make us their willing accomplices.

7

It is precisely the qualities of Richard just enumerated that make his play, so early in Shakespeare's career, the idiosyncratic and powerful piece that it is. And it is precisely the essential qualities of Shakespeare's play that Colley Cibber eliminates. Like Tate's *Lear,* Cibber's *Richard III* has its merits, merits considerable enough to have held the stage as recently at least as Olivier's film.[42] But those improvements are not the essence of his recension. Like Tate, Cibber rewrites the play in order to make it comprehensible to the rational mind. Like Dryden and Otway, he assumes that behavior itself, even when irrational, can be understood according to clear, rational norms. And so, with an adroitness that demands wry admiration, he provides for Richard the motivation that Shakespeare clearly omitted: ambition. A brief description of some of the major changes will make the point.

The famous soliloquy with which Shakespeare opens his play does not appear until Cibber's second scene, and it begins not with Richard's snarling seasonal and solar metaphors but—significantly, as it turns out—with Shakespeare's fourth line, "Now are our Brows bound with victorious Wreaths."[43] It takes a more striking turn at the point at which Shakespeare's Richard declares that since he cannot prove a lover he is "determined to prove a villain/And hate the idle pleasures of these days." In place of those lines Cibber makes a substitution which still lives in Olivier's film:

> Then, since this Earth affords no joy to me,
> But to command, to check, and o'erbear such
> As are of happier Person than my self:
> Why they to me this restless World's but Hell,
> Till this misshapen Trunk's aspiring Head
> Be circl'd in a glorious Diadem!—
> But then 'tis fix'd on such a height; oh! I
> *Must stretch the utmost reaching of my soul.*
> *I'll climb betimes, without remorse or dread.*
>
> (Italics Cibber's)

Two changes are significant. First, Cibber has played down Richard's explanation that his scheme is a compensation for sexual incapacity, perhaps recognizing that Richard is no more convinced by such a claim than we are. But Cibber's second change has larger ramifications for the play: he imputes to Richard the explicit motivation of ambition, of longing for the crown and its perquisites, that by contrast is so vividly missing in Shakespeare.[44]

Never are we allowed to lose sight of that motivation. I need only point to a few of the many instances. In Act II, left alone with Buckingham after the Queen has exclaimed sardonically, "May Heaven prosper all your good Intent," Richard remarks:

> Amen, with all my Heart,—for mine's the Crown;
> And is not that a good one?—
> .   .   .   .
> Now, by St. *Paul,* I feel it here—methinks
> The massy weight on't galls my laden Brow. (P. 99)

Tragic Meanings: The Redactor as Critic

At the end of Act III, like Davenant's Macbeth, he sees himself caught in a dialectical struggle between ambition and conscience, far simpler and more bipolar than anything in Shakespeare:

> Why, now my golden Dream is out!
> Ambition, like an early Friend, throws back
> My Curtains with an eager hand, o'erjoy'd
> To tell me what I dreamt, is true—A Crown!
> Thou bright Reward of ever-daring minds;
> Oh! how thy awful Glory fills my Soul!
> Nor can the means that got thee dim thy Lustre:
> For not Men's Love—Fear pays thee Adoration.
> And Fame, not more, survives from good, than evil,
>   Deeds!
> The acquiring Youth, that fir'd the Ephesian Dome,
> Outlives, in Fame, the pious Fool that rais'd it.
> *Conscience, lie still, more lives must be drain'd;*
> *Crowns got with Blood, must be with Blood maintained.*
>   (P. 113)

In the third scene of the fourth act Richard wrestles again with his conscience. "Wou'd it were done," he exclaims; in the future, when everybody detests the memory of the "crookbacked Tyrant," he consoles himself with another thought that never occurs to Shakespeare's Richard,

>   will not they say too,
> That to possess the Crown, nor Laws divine
> Nor humane stopt my Way?—Why, let 'em say it;
> They can't but say I had the Crown—
> I was not Fool as well as Villain. (Pp. 120–21)

This curious sentiment has already been voiced in the third act, as Richard ends a soliloquy in which he justifies the murder of the Princes in the Tower on the grounds that conscience is a mere "Scare-crow" erected by conscience-less plunderers to frighten others off, and that man is naturally villainous:

> There's not a Slave but has his Share of Villain:
> Why then shall After-Ages think my Deeds
> Inhumane! since my worst are but Ambition.
> *Ev'n all Mankind to some lov'd Ills incline:*
> *Great Men chuse greater Sins, Ambition's mine.*

It is almost as if Cibber can admire Richard more if his crimes have a clear practical goal; it would be foolish, after all, to be merely self-destructive, and in that sense Cibber's Richard, unlike Shakespeare's, is no fool.

Oddly, Cibber does not add the missing coronation scene to the play, perhaps realizing how difficult it would be, both for plausibility and for the turn the plot takes at this point against the tyrant, to show his enemies celebrating his ascension. But later tradition was not even this faithful to Shakespeare. The edition of Cibber's recension published in French's Standard Drama series in New York in the nineteenth century, designed for acting and claiming to be based on the 1846 New York production, lists the following personnel for the "Coronation scene *(discovered):* Two Officers and Sixteen Soldiers of the Royal Guard, Six Banners, Two Pages, holding Shield and Helmet of King Richard, Cardinal, Three Bishops, Four Judges, Four Lawyers, Lord Mayor and Six Aldermen, Six Monks, Friar Beuker, Dr. Shaw, Eight Nobles, &c, &c, &c."[45] Such a scene is perfectly in keeping with Kean's famous acting of Richard III, as described by Hazlitt: "There is at times a sort of tip-toe elevation, an enthusiastic rapture in his expectations of attaining the crown, and at others a gloating expression of sullen delight, as if he already clenched the bauble and held it in his grasp."[46]

As Cibber's Richard falls at Bosworth he breathes his last to Richmond. His last lines, grotesquely, are Northumberland's apocalyptic curse from *2 Henry IV,* I.i. 155ff. But Cibber prefaces this plagiarism with one last reminder of the perfect consistency of Richard's psychology:

Tragic Meanings: The Redactor as Critic

> Perdition catch thy Arm—the Chance is thine.
> But oh! the vast Renown thou hast acquired!
> In conquering *Richard,* does afflict him more
> Than ev'n his Body's parting with his Soul.

Almost more outrageous than the Northumberland lines, these dying words grossly parody Hotspur's last words to Hal. To his final breath this Richard is torn between mounting ambition and agonizing conscience; at the last he recognizes that he has lost the fruits of both. The scheme is far more rational than Shakespeare's, not entertaining for a moment the possibility that the character is really motivated not by such neat polarities but rather by the impulse to destruction and self-destruction that makes Shakespeare's Richard both painful to contemplate and human.

8

As one watches the birth of Shakespearean tragedy in *Richard III,* it is hard not to fancy that one sees the early expression of the same understanding of human behavior that makes the mature tragedies possible. For the play's energy, its power to arouse energetic responses in us, comes from Richard's joy in the familial crimes he engineers with such gusto. These crimes are singularly lacking in the conventional motivation Shakespeare's revisers need to supply. Neither ambition nor the more modern explanation of Richard's behavior as his response to his physical deformity carries adequate conviction. The pleasure of Richard's crimes lies in the acting out of deep intrapsychic motives, in the annihilation of the hero's family and his world. So far has Shakespeare come at the very beginning of his theatrical career.

Only Richard's pleasure and Shakespeare's not yet fully realized power differentiate Richard essentially from Macbeth. Like Richard, Macbeth fools himself and us into thinking that it is the golden round that drives him to regicide. As in *Richard III,* so in *Macbeth* one can point to no single moment when the hero seems able to enjoy the sweet fruition of an earthly crown. But in *Macbeth,* more clearly than in *Richard III,* the regicide's lack of pleasure in his accomplishments is presented not moralistically, as a judgment on evil deeds, but as a defining fact of the deeds themselves. For if Richard at least enjoys the process of manipulation and murder by which he gets where he finally does not want to be, Macbeth's response to his own action is constantly one of horror. As has repeatedly been noticed, he does what he does, not as his wife would do it, willingly in a clear cause, but as if he must do what he does not want to do, and for causes he cannot enunciate. As said earlier, it is Lady Macbeth, never her husband, who speaks of the "golden round" (I.v.28). It is she, not he, who claims that he wants to have what he esteems "the ornament of life." Macbeth, in response, suggests that his own concern is rather with what "may become a man" and with the knowledge that to do what she suggests is to deny or to destroy his own manhood (I.vii.41–47). With singular consistency, in fact, Shakespeare denies Macbeth even a single line that indicates ambition as the spring of his action.[47]

As with the other adaptations we have been examining, Davenant's 1674 redaction of *Macbeth* unwittingly constitutes an astute piece of criticism. Davenant did everything he could to make the play make sense, sensibly (and of course lethally to Shakespeare's play) making Macduff the hero Shakespeare had failed to make of him, conversely turning Macbeth into an uncomplicated villain whom audiences might simply and successfully judge. But Davenant revised not only to simplify the moral response of the audience. He wanted not only to make us despise a man who is obviously wicked, but also to help us understand why Macbeth does such wicked things; and he recognized, as his revisions tell us, that Shakespeare had left that crucial matter obscure. In Davenant's version, as not in Shakespeare, Macbeth's motivation is just what one would expect: ambition.

A bell rings, and Shakespeare's Macbeth goes to do what cannot be undone:

> Hear it not, Duncan, for it is a knell
> That summons thee to heaven or to hell.   (II.1.62–63)

These are the last lines we shall hear Macbeth speak until he emerges with bloody hands, and as always they convey only the anguish he feels at what he must do. But Davenant's Macbeth feels and speaks otherwise:

> O Duncan, hear it not, for 'tis a bell
> That rings my Coronation, and thy Knell.[48]

Ambition is ever his concern. He must choose first between it and virtue, later, as he hears of his wife's distress, between it and love. Thus he shows none of the difficulty Shakespeare's protagonist has, after his encounter with the witches, in formulating the explicit decision to kill Duncan; and afterwards, when Lady Macbeth suggests that he can escape his troubles by resigning his crown, he demonstrates more openly than Shakespeare's hero ever does his desire to be king. What Shakespeare achieved with so much delicacy, the delineation of an evil man as tragic hero through the exploration of his inner process and the demonstration of his purposeless subjection to drives he does not understand and goals he does not want, Davenant has consistently eliminated. No longer must the audience see the tragedy from Macbeth's point of view as well as Duncan's. The hero is Macduff, selflessly concerned with Scotland and rejecting any temptation to ambition. Macbeth is simply the villain of the piece.

Furthermore, Davenant depoliticizes *Macbeth* as successfully as Otway does *Julius Caesar*. The first prerequisite of a healthy polity is the fusion in its central authority of grace, legitimacy, and power. Here as elsewhere Shakespeare suggests the ultimate unattainability of such a polity by splitting the characteristics of the necessary leader, giving to Duncan inner gentleness and divinely sanctioned legitimacy, but to Macbeth the driving force it takes to impose one's will on history. On its political level Shakespeare's play is the tragedy of what happens when these qualities are opposed to one another;[49] it is thus an exploration of precisely the same issue we saw as the heart of the problem in *Henry V*. But in Davenant's play that issue has disappeared. Macduff is every inch a king, Macbeth simply an unsound intruder into a self-sufficient world. Like Tate's *Lear,* the new tragedy is most notable not for its simple and explicit moral but for its efficient elimination of a design that made such a moral so trivial as to be almost irrelevant to what the play was all about.[50]

Just so David Garrick's acting version, which did so much to restore the tragedy to what Shakespeare rather than Davenant intended, needs the explanation of Macbeth's lust for power. Thus Garrick gave to the dying hero a speech that Shakespeare had failed to provide, in which Macbeth can pass judgment on himself and sum up his villainy just as Cibber's Richard had done:

> 'Tis done! the scene of life will quickly close.
> Ambition's vain delusive dreams are fled,
> And now I wake to darkness, guilt and horror.[51]

Perverse though they are, Garrick's lines are steeped in Shakespeare. The "'Tis done" with which they begin echoes the very words Macbeth first speaks as he enters with Duncan's blood on his hands: "I have done the deed." But those words, and everything else Macbeth says in the moments surrounding the murder, tell us that there will be no need, three acts later, to "wake to darkness, guilt and horror": they are the very substance of his act, and he is enticed by no "vain delusive dreams." It is the supreme greatness of Shakespeare's conception that his killer of king and kinsman and self is driven by something darker,

Tragic Meanings: The Redactor as Critic

something deeper and more terrifying, than golden fantasies of royal power.

What then does motivate Macbeth to a chain of murder that leads inevitably to his own inward and worldly destruction? The key, I suggest, is in Lady Macbeth's mysterious explanation for her own surprising sudden inability to kill Duncan: "Had he not resembled / My father as he slept, I had done't," followed immediately by Macbeth's "I have done the deed." Lady Macbeth's compunction, so apparently out of character, acknowledges an unconscious recognition that the killing of a king—of such a king as Duncan, of a kinsman, of the king in such a social structure as that of Scotland—is a form of parricide. And that is what Macbeth knows, and what impels him to his deed.

Only once before the murder does Macbeth allow himself to imagine it with full conceiving of the deed itself. Earlier, confronting the witches, his very syntax is so obscure as to imply his inability to visualize what he is already unconsciously formulating:

> why do I yield to that suggestion
> Whose horrid image doth unfix my hair
> And make my seated heart knock at my ribs?
> . . . .
>
> My thought, whose murther yet is but fantastical,
> Shakes so my single state of man that function
> Is smother'd in surmise, and nothing is
> But what is not. (I.iii.134–142)

Suggestions come in as if from outside, with horrid and unspecified images; thoughts (but not Macbeth) have murders, but they are "fantastical." Only at Forres, in the actual presence of the gracious King, does Macbeth speak more honestly and explicitly with himself.

> Stars, hide your fires,
> Let not light see my black and deep desires;
> The eye wink at the hand; yet let that be

> Which the eye fears, when it is done, to see.
> (I.iv.50–53)

But why now? What has changed? In this ceremonial scene, more than anywhere else, Macbeth plays the role of ideal filial subject—"our duties / Are to your throne and state children and servants"—spelling out what would be a moving credo of monarchical ideology were it not entirely ironic. What enables Macbeth, almost as he enunciates the familial ideal which underlies the structure of the state, to admit to himself at last his readiness to strike down the head and center of that state?

Only one thing happens in this scene: Duncan ritualistically announces that Malcolm will be his heir. Playing the part of loving son to his symbolic father and real kinsman, Macbeth hears Duncan convey his blessings to another son. Interestingly, though there is no suggestion in the play that Duncan's act is anything but proper, Shakespeare's source told him that the King's historical prototype illegally invoked the rule of primogeniture in a Scotland governed otherwise, thus at least partially justifying the rebellion against him.[52] (Similarly in *Julius Caesar,* while shading Brutus's murder of Caesar with emotions generally recognized as parricidal, Shakespeare suppresses his source's suggestion that Brutus was, or at any rate thought himself, Caesar's natural son.) Significantly Shakespeare omits any hint that Duncan's act is illegal, and "Macbeth's ambition," in the words of Geoffrey Bullough, "therefore becomes wilder and less well-founded."[53] For Macbeth it is the very act of treating Malcolm as a favorite son that triggers a murderous impulse, providing the context for the explicit resolve noted above.

> The Prince of Cumberland! that is a step
> On which I must fall down, or else o'er leap,
> For in my way it lies. Stars, hide your fires. . . .

Since, as Bullough observes, "the reasons why the nomination of Malcolm as heir would so disturb him are not brought out . . . Macbeth's claims to the throne by his own birth and through his wife are not mentioned,"[54] one must infer irrational motives. It is as if Macbeth decides to kill Duncan out of the rage of a disappointed sibling. Not that the succession or its announcement is the cause of Macbeth's action: he has already felt the attraction of the deed; rather that this moment defines and crystallizes a parricidal emotion that resides already in his deepest being.

Is it not this unconscious hatred of a father that motivates Macbeth? Is not the terror of the play the fact that its hero, morally as aware as any character in his world, better at judging himself than any of those who witness his crimes, is driven so inexorably to a deed he does not want but feels compelled to commit? As Traversi brilliantly argued, Macbeth strikes out to destroy what he above all others recognizes as "the source of all the benefits which flow from his person to those who surround him," and he does so while "groping in the bottomless pit of psychological and spiritual darkness," and does so "in a state of hallucination."[55] Drawn forward by the dagger of the mind he sees before him, Macbeth fantasies himself as Murder personified, who

> with his stealthy pace,
> With Tarquin's ravishing [strides], towards his design
> Moves like a ghost. (II.i.52–56)

The analogy is multiply apt, of course: a royal crime in a bedroom at night; the aggression of violence against an almost feminine helplessness; an act whose ultimate victim is its perpetrator. But most powerful in the image is the sense of the crime as one of lust: of an act dictated not by the impulse of ambition, which seemed so rational to Shakespeare's redactors in literary periods less able to acknowledge the darker sources of human action, but by a drive as fundamental and as irrational as that of sex.[56] Almost out of control, excitedly describing the murdered King to the sleepers of the house, Macbeth speaks moments after the crime of "th'expedition of my violent love"

(II.iii.110); like much else that he says here, he comes—as his wife's collapse suggests she understands—too close to the truth. The true horror of *Macbeth* is the suggestion that the nihilistic criminality that we normally associate with the pursuit of power and control may stem ultimately not from such relatively positive goals but from the very hatred of that which has given us life.[57]

The psychoanalytic reading to which I have just pointed is, of course, very much a product of our own age. Much of the most invigorating and plausible work on Shakespeare is now being produced by critics with a Freudian orientation who, unlike some of the early psychoanalytic critics, unlike Freud himself, study literature with an awareness of the ways in which their own limited perspective draws strength from and illuminates a comprehensive view based on a variety of techniques and modes of perception.[58] Such critics have been demonstrating how richly susceptible Shakespeare's understanding of character is to psychoanalytic exploration, and therefore how much Shakespeare seems to have anticipated of modern psychological discovery. The work of these critics is as valuable as any now being done, and it seems only at the beginning of its long march. I do not want, therefore, to suggest any dissatisfaction with it.

On the other hand, it can all too easily be charged that such a claim as, no doubt inspired by the intellectual climate, I have made about Macbeth's motivation is a new reduction invented to replace an old one. Let me confess to the charge. What I have said about Macbeth seems to me unmistakably there to be found. But it was put there not by a twentieth-century author trained in the discipline of Freudian psychology, but by a seventeenth-century dramatist who could not have found any equivalent of that discipline in his culture. What we find in *Macbeth,* therefore, is not the confident demonstration of a familiar syndrome, but rather an obscure hinting of motivations that lie buried too deeply to be susceptible of seventeenth-century explanation. To be sure, Shakespeare's psychological canniness reveals him as one of the great inventors of human self-understanding. Observing personality in life and books, he may have come to certain conclusions about what we might describe as the nature and etiology of psychosis, but as a playwright he does not set out to teach lessons in psychology. He seems to have been unable to imagine a character, and particularly a protagonist created during the period of the great tragedies, without imagining him fully, embodying in him his shrewdest perceptions about human motivation. As the author of *Macbeth*, however, rather than simply as the creator of Macbeth, he has aims that are artistic as well as psychological.

The primary fact about *Macbeth* that Davenant's redaction can teach us is not that Macbeth is oedipal rather than ambitious, but that his behavior is based on unconscious motives which he is incapable of knowing. What an audience takes away is not a lesson in psychopathology but a demonstration of the inscrutability of human behavior. And that is suggested, in *Macbeth* as in *Richard III*, by the fact that the psychological explanation does not explain everything. It does not explain the witches, seen by Banquo as well as by Macbeth, or the truth of prophecies; it does not explain why Richard III was born with his teeth, or why the owl shrieked at his birth and "hideous tempest shook down trees" (*3 Henry VI*, V.vi.46). I am tempted to believe that if Shakespeare had had access to a fully worked out psychoanalytic theory of human behavior, he would have employed it theatrically with as much skepticism as he seems to give to other explanatory paradigms. The understanding of character suggested by *Macbeth* is only secondarily psychoanalytic; more important is the implication that ultimate motivation is often crucially obscure, and that it can work, in the world as seen with a tragic vision, through a mysterious but definitive complicity with a metaphysical universe. In the worlds of *Macbeth* and *Richard III*, in the universe of Shakespearean tragedy, human behavior is governed by unknown and unknowable forces from within and without; it is no more reducible to the exclusive formulations of modern psychoanalysis than it is to those of seventeenth-century theology. If we may learn from Shakespeare's redactors that the unconscious figures more in his view of character than they want to acknowledge, we must also learn that the ultimate ineffability of human motivation is close to the meaning of Shakespearean tragedy.

9

In *Timon of Athens,* most critics agree, Shakespeare failed to realize his design.[59] Rather than involving its audience fruitfully in the pull between the possible understandings its experience can produce, the play invites us to reject both extravagant phases, philanthropic and misanthropic, of its hero's life. In place of complementarity we experience confusion. Whatever their cause or function, however, it is the ambiguities of Shakespearean tragedy that we have watched Restoration revisers excising, and in *Timon of Athens, or the Man-Hater,* Thomas Shadwell manages, by normalizing his original, to make neat and smug entertainment of Shakespeare's aborted tragedy.[60] Like Macbeth and Lear, Timon is simplified, in this instance made into a sentimental paragon, the cause, through Alcibiades' sympathy, for the reform of Athens. One critic has argued that Shadwell supplies the richness Shakespeare omitted, making a play of a sketch.[61] But in fact the addition of detail serves once again to remove complexity. The most notable novelty consists of two women who turn the play into Fletcherian tragedy. Timon abandons his beloved and chaste Evandra to plan marriage to the fickle Melissa, who deserts him with his friends when the money runs out. Evandra, however, follows him into the woods to dig for roots with him, and watches happily as he moralistically rejects Melissa when, suspecting he has hidden wealth, she comes to court him in the wilderness. When Timon dies, Evandra stabs herself so that she may die with him, and when Melissa courts her first love, Alcibiades, on his triumphant return, he too rejects her because of her cruelty to Timon. As a sentimental melodrama, Shadwell's play is more purposefully engineered than Shakespeare's; in the manner of the other adaptations, it manages by syllogistic structure to eradicate much of what is Shakespearean in the original design.

The same deftness and clarity of intent make the last adaptation I am going to cite an almost shocking instance of the process I have been describing. Shakespeare's *Coriolanus* so epitomizes his previous tragic technique as almost to parody it. Opposing private to public honor and, by identifying the one with Coriolanus and the other with his mother, suggesting that each is authentically Roman, the play demonstrates that honor is a meaningless and destructive concept in politics without which the polity cannot survive. The hero is the only idealist yet the man most obviously and deeply driven by neurotic impulse rather than ideas, the most patriotic of Romans yet the betrayer of both Rome and the Volscians to whom he turns. Characters are so profoundly motivated by class interest that a harmonious society seems unattainable, but no single class offers a solution to perpetual civil strife. If critical cant held it to be the duties of art to please and instruct, the bleak and uncompromising pessimism of Shakespeare's late tragedy strained both these categories to their limits.

But in *The Ingratitude of a Commonwealth: or, the Fall of Caius Martius Coriolanus*[62] Tate corrected these faults. As his title indicates, Tate has a message, which he spells out in his fawning epistle-dedicatory to a grandson of the martyred Charles I: "The Moral therefore of these scenes being to recommend Submission and Adherence to Establisht Lawful Power, which in a word is Loyalty" (A2ᵛ). The Tory's ideal monarch, Coriolanus is aristocratically proud, but reasonable and capable of bending in the interests, identical for Tate, of class and country. The loving father of a bathetic son, he is normal and admirable by all but the perverted standards of the bestial rabble. With the same skill he manifested in *The History of King Lear,* Tate purges *Coriolanus* of its central problematics. His ultimate expedient is precisely the one chosen by Otway, the displacing of political and characterological issues by sex: Aufidius's role, it turns out, originates in a frustrated love for Virgilia which sours to a desire to rape her before her husband's eyes.

Rather than adduce other such large-scale changes in Shakespeare's design, I can demonstrate the clarity of Tate's revision by pointing to a few of the apparently trivial improvements he makes at the beginning in the interest of unequivocal statement. The first occurs in line 14: where Shakespeare's hungry citizen observes, "What authority surfeits on would relieve us," Tate omits the allusion to authority; the class attack is gone. Second, the bewildering multiplicity of praiseworthy and contemptible motives suggested by the citizens as the causes of Shakespeare's hero's behavior, all of which turn out to be accurate, is drastically reduced to one remark about pride; gone is the typical Shakespearean preparation for the first entrance of a hero, raising conflicting expectations and building the foundation for ambivalent responses throughout.[63] Third, in arguing with the outraged citizens Menenius is allowed to keep his antiplebeian tale of the belly but made to drop his ironic picture of the violent course of the Roman state as with relentless power it drives through history. Fourth, Martius's prophetic identification with Rome's enemy Aufidius—"And were I anything but what I am, / I would wish me only he" (I.i.231–32)—is dropped for a simple statement that he likes fighting such a strong enemy. Fifth, Martius's misanthropic delight that the outbreak of war will kill off the musty superfluity of his homeland is expurgated. And finally, when after winning a battle and accepting the title of Coriolanus the hero asks one favor, that he be allowed to repay the kindness of a poor old man, Tate's Coriolanus does not forget his benefactor's name. In a word, where Shakespeare designs his play to depict Coriolanus's moral superiority as simultaneous and identical with his mortifying limitations, Tate eliminates every embarrassing touch that might qualify the audience's admiration, making of a tragedy that verges on satire a virtual saint's life. Once again the result is a play so efficiently meaningful that it is no more than melodrama.[64]

10

The adaptations and imitations we have examined have suggested some insights into Shakespeare's tragedies. I should like to point to some further implications of the group taken as a whole.

The first is a suggestion about the nature of tragedy, particularly as Shakespeare practiced and refined that art. As much modern theorizing about painting and music has demonstrated, conflict between the elements of which it is built is virtually a defining quality of the work of art. In a verbal art the conflicting elements are often, though never exclusively, conceptual, so that literary critics, New or not, have agreed for some time that tension, paradox, ambiguity, and irony—all of them special forms of conceptual conflict expressed in aesthetic forms—are essential elements of authentic literary art. I have called the most characteristic and central kind of conflict in Shakespeare's work "complementarity," an approach to experience in which, as I have suggested here in discussing a few of the plays, radically opposed and equally total commitments to the meaning of life coexist in a single harmonious vision.[65] Shakespeare's complementarity is not restricted to his tragedies, but is rather a crucial feature of almost all his work, both dramatic and nondramatic, and I have suggested that something like complementarity figures in much of the greatest literature of our entire tradition. (The word itself is borrowed from the physicists Bohr and Oppenheimer, who see complementarity as a widespread and fundamental element in human thought.)

But I suspect that it is tragedy, of all literary forms, which most depends on complementarity for its meaning and effectiveness. For though much literature is based on or draws its energy from the play between mutually exclusive points of view, tragedy produces in its audience the most threatening and moving apprehension of the perception that life essentially demands a choice between alternatives while making that choice impossible. The difference between tragedy and other forms is in part one of kind: unlike comedy, for example, it is not concerned with escape or reconciliation, and unlike melodrama, as Heilman notes, it achieves its "total view" by seeing, without taking sides, "the diversity of claims and urgencies that divide humanity,"[66] of the imperatives that constitute the nature of man. But the difference is at least as much one of degree: the intensity of tragedy demands that audiences experience pain in their encounter with a subject matter that is in itself not radically different from that of other forms. Shakespeare's tragedies define the genre for us; whatever successes his redactors achieved they achieved by making the plays into something other than tragedy, something more reducible to rational equation.

The second implication is historical. In a fine little poem about Thomas Hobbes's return to Cromwell's England, John Hollander suggests the postcataclysmic weariness of a country not yet past its troubles but already headed towards the stability—ironically not that of Cromwell's order—which would soon be transforming its institutions and its life:

> When I returned at last from Paris hoofbeats pounded
> Over the harsh and unrelenting road;
> It was cold, the snow high; I was old, and the winter
> Sharp, and the dead mid-century sped by

Tragic Meanings: The Redactor as Critic

> In ominous, blurred streaks as, brutish, the wind
>   moaned
> Among black branches. I rode through a kind
> Of graceless winter nature, bled of what looked like
>   life.
> My vexing horse threw me. If it was not safe
> In England yet, or ever, that nowhere beneath the
>   grey
> Sky would be much safer seemed very plain.[67]

The Stuart restoration nine years after Hobbes's return signals an end as well as a beginning. Not, certainly, an end to partisan strife, class warfare, political and theological disputation; but a closing of the deep divisions that had culminated inevitably in a civil war such as England has not experienced since.

Once dominated by wishful assumptions about the stability of the Elizabethan establishment, our understanding of the political, intellectual, and religious life of England has increasingly encompassed an awareness that the civil war was the result of considerably more than half a century of social breakdown on every level. In this kind of crisis the opposed ideas which normally coexist more or less comfortably in society and the individual become critical issues, the people of all sorts find themselves driven to absolutism of one kind or another: revolution and counterrevolution are, after all, only the ultimate expression of radical reductions. In Shakespeare's day conflicts that had been voiced throughout much of the sixteenth century tended increasingly to polarize those who favored one side or the other. As long as such conflicts raged within the limits of a society still relatively stable, they made tragedy possible. When they grew too strong for society to be able to contain them, tragedy was one of the first casualties of what ensued.

Every aspect of Renaissance thought and life is more deeply conflicted than its counterpart after the watershed. Sixteenth- and early seventeenth-century men and women were constrained to endure fundamental contradictions masked only superficially and with less success as the actual eruption of armed conflict drew near: contradictions between monarchical absolutism and anti-monarchical iconoclasm in politics, between fideism and atheism and radical reformism in religion, between the irreconcilable interests of classes, between free will and Calvinistic determinism, between conceptions of heroism—that is, of ideal humanity—as proudly individualistic and as humbly selfless, between reason and intuitive process. Paradox is more than a matter of style in Renaissance literature.[68] Whatever their ultimate commitments, Donne and Milton and Herbert, Chapman and Webster, all, like Shakespeare, built their achievements on the acknowledgment of the impossible simultaneity of contradictory realities. In the greatest works of the period, most profoundly perhaps in *Paradise Lost,* those realities are made to cohere in a vision in which everything has its place and a single point of view reconciles apparent differences, but the tentativeness of the solution, the heroic effort it took to create and maintain it, is evinced both by the complexity of our response to, say, Milton's Satan or Marlowe's Faustus or Shakespeare's Coriolanus, and by the unceasing disagreements of critics as to their authors' real attitudes toward their creations.

The animating contradictions of Renaissance literature may reflect the kind of ferment that precedes the scientific revolution described by Thomas Kuhn,[69] when the intellectual life of a period consists in trying to reconcile disruptive new knowledge with established overviews which no longer comprehend it but cannot yet be abandoned. It might further be argued that in the politics of the later seventeenth century, as in post-Newtonian science, a new gestalt offered a satisfactory point of view from which the old conflicts could be seen as resolvable. This hypothesis might help to explain why in Dryden and Otway, for example, the contest between reason and passion is so much more clearly formulated than it was in the plays they imitated, and why it is so foregone a conclusion. As the new understanding of life leads to well-made and well-meaning plays, the new picture of man leads to a confident definition of character, succinctly expressed by Dryden: "A character . . . is a composition of qualities which are not contrary to one another in the same person."[70] This rubric cannot accommodate the self-destructiveness Davenant has helped us see in Macbeth; it keeps out more of Shakespeare's great characters than it admits.

The third implication of our examination is about audiences. Considering the successes of both Shakespeare and Tate, one could hardly fail to draw the inference that people go to the theater at different times for different reasons; and one might legitimately hope that by analyzing the characteristic drama of a period one might infer much about the psychology of those who applauded it. The evidence provided by plays themselves suggests that the audience of Shakespearean tragedy went to the theater to find ways of relieving the cultural pressures under which it lived, while the audience of Restoration tragedy could scarcely have found its experience in the theater so personally important. If Shakespearean theater reflects spiritual crisis in both artist and audience, Restoration theater suggests the inner comfort of a less essentially conflicted period.

Such tentative conclusions are hypothetical, and certainly beyond the scope of the present study to prove or even to press. Whether or not they are valid, however, it is an undeniable fact that Shakespearean tragedy, as understood from the perspective of the Restoration, constitutes an extraordinary balancing act in which the theater explores the most mystifying contradictions in human experience; and, unlike later attempts by dramatists and literary critics alike to explain away the mysteries, it has come down to us not only as our heritage but as our comtemporary.

4

Both/And: Nature and Illusion
in the Romances

Talking about Shakespeare's last plays, critics often tend to
divide into opposite camps, though their opposition man-
ifests itself more often in ignoring the existence of the
other camp than in the controversy that marks the interpretation of *Henry V*. Once again, examination of interpretative reduction can lead us both to what is problematic
in the plays and to a fuller understanding of them.

On one level each of the last plays is concerned with the
creation of a world that can be interpreted as we interpret
the world of any of the earlier plays. In that world, as in
any Shakespearean world, character and destiny are aspects of a cosmos whose laws control the action of the
play, and our illusion is that we are participating in a life
that has its own full and peculiar integrity. Thus, when in
The Winter's Tale we see the tragedy of middle age dissolve
into the comedy of youth at a sheep-shearing, we remember that before the tragic events, through the dark
backward and abysm of time, Leontes and Polixenes had
spent a childhood like the childhood of Florizel and Perdita, "as twinn'd lambs that did frisk i' th' sun,/ And bleat
the one at th' other," and we become aware of a world in
which time moves cyclically in a process of eternal re-
newal. To take another instance from the same episode:
"Have you thought," Camillo asks Florizel, resolved for
flight, "on/ A place whereto you'll go?" "Not any yet," the
boy replies:

Both/And: Nature and Illusion in the Romances

> But as th' unthought-on accident is guilty
> To what we wildly do, so we profess
> Ourselves to be the slaves of chance, and flies
> Of every wind that blows; (IV.iv.537–41)

and we remember again. We remember that Polixenes began the trouble when he decided he had to leave Sicilia because of "sneaping winds" (I.ii.13) that might be blowing in the court of his Bohemia; we remember that Leontes, describing with ironic accuracy the surrender of his reason to his will, declared: "I am a feather for each wind that blows" (II.iii.154); we remember that the winds carried the infant Perdita to the seacoast of Bohemia; and we recognize that inscrutably but unmistakably the winds of the world and the winds of human passion are identical, and that more perhaps than in plays of other kinds nature and man's nature are one. On this level the play is a window looking out to a profound and subtle view of the real world. But on another level something else is happening: the Bohemian coast on which Perdita lands, Shakespeare and his audience know just as well as we, exists only in the poet's mind. Each of the last plays calls attention to the fact that what we are experiencing is art, not life, whether by the use of such awkward playwright surrogates as Time and Gower, or the incessant allusions to stage performance, or the drama of real characters in fairy-tale gardens, or sudden changes from one genre to another, or in *The Tempest* the clear implication that Prospero is in some way to be thought of as analogous to the author of the play.

It has become increasingly fashionable in recent years to emphasize the latter, the "metadramatic" or self-reflexive signals in the romances, and in doing so to interpret the plays as "about" play-making.[1] Many critics concentrate on these signals and discuss the "romances" as autobiographical or as reflections on "the idea of the play." Others ignore them and profitably analyze the plays' illusory worlds in the dramatic, rather than the metadramatic, terms they demand with equal urgency. Both approaches have pro-

Both/And: Nature and Illusion in the Romances

duced extraordinarily good criticism. Both of them are reductive.[2]

Two instances will illustrate my point. As early as 1947 Northrop Frye, pointing to the self-conscious unreality of the "world of fairies, dreams, disembodied souls, and pastoral lovers" that comprise the world of Shakespeare's comedies, noted that "the famous speech of Prospero about the dream nature of reality applies equally to Milan and the enchanted island," and argued that *The Tempest* leads us to a "detachment of the spirit born of two illusory realities." I do not want to quarrel with Frye's convincing assertion about what *The Tempest* makes us realize about the reality of the "real" world, the dream nature of our own Milans. What does call for comment, however, is the conclusion he draws: "We need not ask whether this [detachment of the spirit] brings us into a higher order of existence or not, for the question of existence is not relevant to poetry."[3] Eighteen years later, in *A Natural Perspective,* Frye continues to insist that the only true subject of the plays is their own art: "In comedy and romance the story seeks its own end instead of holding the mirror up to nature. Consequently comedy and romance are so obviously conventionalized that a serious interest in them soon leads to an interest in convention itself."[4] Thus, in *The Winter's Tale* the world we see is

> the world symbolized by nature's power of renewal; it is the world we want; it is the world we hope our gods would want for us if they were worth worshiping. But it is "monstrous to our human reason," according to Paulina, and its truth "is so like an old tale that the verity of it is in strong suspicion." Such things happen in stories, not in life, and the world *The Winter's Tale* leaves us with is neither an object of knowledge nor of belief.[5]

My second instance is Frank Kermode's justly admired introduction to *The Tempest.* If Frye argues that such reality as the romances imply leads us to a world that exists only in poetry, Kermode discusses art in *The Tempest* exclusively as an aspect of the nature dramatized by the play. The force of the play, he contends, is in its exemplification of his definition of "romance": "a mode of exhibiting the action of magical and moral laws in a version of human life so selective as to obscure, for the special purpose of concentrating attention on these laws, the fact that in reality their force is intermittent and only fitfully glimpsed."[6] In this view, the arbitrary and obtrusive conventions of the romances serve to make the plays seem normative, to make us feel that because they generalize and abstract life they are realer than reality. As Frye must deny that the plays attempt to lead us out to the world, so Kermode simply dismisses the "autobiographical interpretation" according to which the plays point inward to themselves as art.[7]

Frye and Kermode are worth citing not because they are wrong but because they are on the whole so right about these plays. The polarity of art and nature is so richly embodied in *Pericles, Cymbeline, The Winter's Tale,* and *The Tempest* as to make possible full and coherent explanations of each play in terms suggesting Shakespeare's exclusive concern with the nature of art or the artifice of nature. But, as we have seen in considering earlier plays, the simpler the explanation, the more likely it is to reduce the play to its schema.[8] A fuller reading of these plays must acknowledge the importance in them of both nature and art.

1

The double view of reality imposed on the audience of Shakespeare's romances has its analogues elsewhere in imaginative literature, and I propose to illuminate it by going, not like Frye to other Shakespearean comedy or like Kermode to Renaissance speculations on nature, but rather to the final works of one of the great masters of the twentieth century, which in their technique, their subject matter, their attitude toward that matter, and their effect on an audience reveal an extraordinary affinity with Shakespeare's final plays. Thomas Mann did not call *The Holy Sinner, The Confessions of Felix Krull, Confidence Man,* and *The Black Swan* "romances"; but Shakespeare did not use the term either. What we are talking about is not a genre but a kind of art produced by a certain kind of artist at the end of a life of mastery. That Mann's novels differ from Shakespeare's plays in tone as much as they do makes the essential similarities of the two bodies of work all the more extraordinary. By looking at some points of correspondence between Mann's late novels and Shakespeare's late plays I hope to suggest a new way of bridging the useful but restrictive approaches of the critical schools represented by Frye and Kermode.[9]

Written only four years before Mann's death in 1955, *The Holy Sinner* is a redaction of Hartmann von Aue's *Gregorius vom Stein.* Nothing could better illustrate its appropriateness to a consideration of Shakespeare's last plays than a brief summary of the plot. Wiligis and Sibylla, twin children of the widowed Duke of Flaundres and Artoys, consumate a sudden access of incestuous affection on the night of their father's death. Their affair produces its predictable fruit. Wiligis leaves Christian realms, entrusting his pregnant sister to the Baron Eisengrein. When her boy is born, Sibylla and the Baron's wife persuade Eisengrein to entrust him to the seas in a cask laden with assorted medieval treasures. Wiligis dies; Sibylla copes with courtship from men unacquainted with her secret; and the baby, found by fishermen on the shores of the island of Saint Dunstan, is brought to the saintly abbot Gregorius, who gives his name, abbreviated to Grigorss, to the child and finds a foster home for him with the fisherman Wiglaf and his wife Mahaute. Educated by the monk, Grigorss reaches a naturally aristocratic young manhood, instinctively chivalrous and mournful. When he is sev-

enteen, an unsolicited fight with another of Mahaute's
children leads to her angry revelation of Grigorss's mysterious arrival, and the young man leaves to seek his fortunes
in the world. Even those who know neither the novel nor
its source will scarcely be surprised to learn that the self-
styled Knight of the Fish promptly makes his unconsicous
way to a duel in which he defeats one Roger the Invincible,
who for years has sought the hand of Sibylla, and that the
upshot is Grigorss's marriage to his own mother. After
three years the couple learn the truth, and Grigorss, leaving his wife-mother-aunt with two daughters and a sermon
on atonement, dons rags and leg-iron, persuades a fisherman to ferry him to a bare rock at sea, and spends seventeen penitent years exposed to the elements, locked
into the fetal position, nourished by a curious milk produced by the rock until he turns into a tiny hedgehog-like
creature. In the last sequence of the novel, a crisis occurs
in the papal succession, and inspired respectively by a
vision and a miracle two Romans set out to find the true
successor: one Gregorius. Finding the fisherman who took
Grigorss to the rock, the Romans watch as he discovers a
key in the fish he is cleaning. The key, it turns out, is to the
leg-iron locked onto Grigorss by the fisherman seventeen
years ago; at that time the fisherman had thrown the key
into the waves, swearing he would believe his odd pas-
senger was genuinely a holy penitent only if he should see
the key again. The discovery leads rapidly to the restoration of Grigorss's human form, to his investiture as Pope,
and to a reunion with his penitent mother, now promoted
to Abbess, and with his daughters by her, who, as Clemens, the narrator, points out, are the Pope's nieces; and
the novel ends in a radiant mood of reconciliation and
praise of God.

Mann's romance is as rich and complex as the impulse
that turned the author of *Doctor Faustus* toward that
novel's matter in his eighth decade, and I can only hint
now at those elements of *The Holy Sinner* that make it

impossible when reading it not to think of Shakespeare's last phase. First of all there is the material: the outlandish saint's life, a fairy-tale of familial separations, reunions, and sexual problems, baldly presented in all its absurdity, yet simultaneously in a lovingly realized ambiance of an authentic romance world replete with courts and tourneys, fishermen's huts and sparkling seas, hidden bedrooms, hunts, and anachronistic Toledo swords. It is a story hard for its own participants to believe without faith. Thus, when one of the churchmen who find Grigorss on the rock worries about how he will be received when he returns with a hedgehog in his bosom and crowns it with the papal tiara, Grigorss asks him to believe that the heaven that has nourished him on rock's milk will certainly restore him to man's estate; and with equal explicitness the narrator requests faith of the audience as the penitent is returned to his original condition by the sacramental function of the ordinary bread and wine he eats on the return trip. Demanding that we assent to a preposterous story so bewitchingly narrated as frequently to move us, Mann uses his tale to awaken us to the magical beauty of the ordinary: the fish with its belly cut open in the hut, the crowds in the streets of Rome, the love of man and woman. Grigorss's rebirth is absurd and tongue-in-cheek yet deeply affecting; parallel to his earlier "birth out of the wild waves,"[10] it reminds us as well of Joseph's rebirth from the well into which he had been cast, which almost two decades earlier Mann had detailed with a similar implication of the spiritual rebirth that is the central experience of all lives worth celebrating—those that William James called the "twice-born." As in Shakespeare's last plays, then, a self-consciously primitive narrative serves to provide an experience simultaneously entertaining and evocative of the self's inner life, and does so by making us regard its material all at once as mere storytelling and realer than life itself.

Both/And: Nature and Illusion in the Romances

The virtuosity and charm of the narrative do not alone account for the excitement it arouses. At least as important is the sense Mann gives of the force that drives the events of the story. In the world of *The Holy Sinner* every event has three causes. To Wiligis, to Sibylla, to Grigorss, the action is a sequence of disasters apparently unmitigated until the end, but their medium is a plot in which each disaster proves to be part of a providential scheme. Life for the novel's characters has some of the qualities of a dream, in which circumstances move toward unforeseen but inevitable ends and the dreamer knows least the meaning of his own actions. Grigorss's sin is the foundation of his blessing; we shall learn later that at the crucial moment he knows deeply that he is committing an act of incest, yet watching him at that moment we see him so out of touch with the realities of his inner life that in a more important sense he does not know what he is doing. Such a welter of knowing and not knowing, sinfulness yet help-lessness before impulses not of their own making, of suicidal steps toward their ultimate rebirth touches the characterizations of Prospero, Pericles, and Leontes. Even the fisherman's angry toss of the key turns out to be a providential act which leads to the discovery of the peni-tent, who, it turns out, has grown small enough anyway to have slipped out of the leg-iron in which his antagonist had thought to imprison him. Thus two causes, one in the motions of the spirit and the other in the motions of the world, turn out to be identical.

But I said *three* causes. The third is the narrator, and here the analogy to Shakespeare is most striking. As God controls the world represented, so Clemens tells us he controls the story. At the beginning the bells of Rome are ringing wildly. At the end we will learn that the occasion of their ringing is the three-day coronation of Pope Greg-ory, from which point the garrulous narrator looks back to the story's beginning. Who rings the bells? he asks at the outset, and well he might: the bellringers have run into the street to see the new pope, the ropes hang slack. The ringing of the bells is a miracle, like the other miracles that have brought Grigorss to his final glory, additional proof of the operation of God's grace in the world. But Clemens has another answer to his question:

> Who is ringing the bells? . . . . Shall one say that *nobody* rings them? No, only an ungrammatical head, without logic, would be capable of the utterance. "The bells are ringing": that means they are rung, and let the bell-chambers be never so empty.—So who is ringing the bells of Rome?—*It is the spirit of story-telling.* . . . He it is that says: "All the bells were ringing"; and, in consequence, it is he who rings them. So spiritual is this spirit, and so abstract that grammatically he can be talked of only in the third person and simply referred to as "It is he." And yet he can gather himself into a person, and be incarnate in somebody who speaks in him and says: "I am he. I am the spirit of story-telling, who, sitting in his time-place, namely in the library of the cloister of St. Gall in Allemannenland, . . . tells this story for entertainment and exceptional edification; in that I begin with its grace-abounding end and ring the bells of Rome; *id est,* report that on that day of processional entry they all together began to ring of themselves." (Pp. 4–5; italics Mann's)

Who rings the bells? Who chooses the "chosen" of Mann's German title, *Der Erwählte?* Providence does; the narrator does: there is no distinction.

Three years earlier Mann had focused *Doctor Faustus* on its narrator as well as its hero; in *The Holy Sinner* the split focus is even more important. As we respond to the events of the real world projected by the narrative, we repeatedly find the narrator calling attention to his role; God's manipulation of that world is identical to the storyteller's manipulation of the plot. Let me cite two characteristic moments. "Now behold how God brought it to pass, and with the utmost dexterity contrived against Himself, that the Lord Grimald's grandson, the child of the bad children, should come happily to shore in a cask."[11] We need hardly have noticed that earlier Clemens had taken credit for imagining the loading of the cask himself (p. 68)—once again the multiple causes of narrated events—to see the implication that the life which is the subject of the plot is a work of art contrived by God, a comedy: even a joke, in which at the end the new pope can meet his ex-wife and call her "Mother" and she with equal accuracy can call him "Father." The second instance is an apotheosis. In that final scene, Grigorss and Sibylla confess what we have long suspected: when they broke the taboo, each of them was darkly aware of what he was doing: in pretending to be simply lovers, they "play-acted," Grigorss says,[12]— ironically the interview occurs in a chapter entitled "The Audience"—and later: "We thought to offer God an entertainment."[13]

Life as an entertainment for God! This, I propose, is the vision of the romances.[14] It is a vision rather than a theme, a way of seeing, a mode of comprehension and response, and it explains the dual focus on the presentational and the representational with which we have been concerned here. It explains the otherwise inexplicable insistence in the plays that the life presented as a version of our lives is itself like art, the recurrent suggestion that as people who act we are like actors in a play, the haunting analogies between Propero's mastery and Shakespeare's, the simultaneous presentation of irremediable evil in a context in which grace triumphs and the potency of evil becomes itself part of an enchanting landscape, a spectacle to amuse us as well as an image of our lives' reality.

> Go play, boy, play. Thy mother plays, and I
> Play too, but so disgrac'd a part, whose issue
> Will hiss me to my grave,

says Leontes, and later Hermione, defending herself against a grief that is "more/Than history can pattern, though devis'd/And play'd to take spectators," rightly guesses that because "pow'rs divine/Behold our human actions," her play must have a happy ending. "The dignity of this act was worth the audience [a pun identical to Mann's] of kings and princes, for by such was it acted."

> Good Paulina,
> Lead us from hence, where we may leisurely
> Each one demand, and answer to his part
> Perform'd in this wide gap of time since first
> We were dissever'd.[15]

"We thought to offer God an entertainment."

2

"How inventive life is! Lending substance to airy nothings, it brings our childhood dreams to pass." Neither a comment on Prospero's farewell to his art nor a passage from *The Holy Sinner,* that remark is made by Felix Krull as he contemplates his successful parlaying of a Parisian waiter's role into his triumphant assumption of the name and fortunes of the Marquis de Venosta.[16] Begun in 1911, laid down as if forever, resumed only a year before Mann's death without the slightest flicker of a change in tone, *The Confessions of Felix Krull* spans a creative lifetime of obsession with the artist's role. In what may turn out to be the comic masterpiece of the twentieth century, Mann plays in the mode of art and life a set of variations which could justify lengthy analysis, and I shall merely indicate schematically some of the novel's features that, taken with what I have been observing at greater length in *The Holy Sinner,* point to a new perspective on Shakespeare's romances.

A parodic version of Mann's earlier Joseph, making his miraculous way through an unmiraculous world by a combination of comic shrewdness, protean ability to transform himself in a never-ending series of impostures, and an unfailing luck that seems somehow complementary to his own capacity, Felix Krull is the last and most complex of his author's artist-heroes. His resemblance to Shakespeare's Autolycus is nothing less than astonishing. Both rogues glory in an amoral mastery of the raw materials of life by force of their artistry as well as in their outrageous yet delightful playing on the weaknesses of all those who become grist for their mill. "My father nam'd me Autolycus," boasts Shakespeare's confidence man, "who being, as I am, litter'd under Mercury, was likewise a snapper-up of unconsidered trifles" (IV.iii.24–26); and if the genealogy puts us in mind of Odysseus, grandson of another Autolycus, as still another analogue to a hero who triumphs repeatedly over a comic world through a constantly self-transforming wit, it points more significantly at an identification with Hermes, patron alike of artists and thieves.

Introducing him at a tender age to the world of classical antiquity, Krull's godfather, Schimmelpreester, had cited the case of Phidias to teach him the identity of artist and thief,[17] and the ready student had promptly realized the appropriateness of the lesson in his first encounter with the shabbiness that hides backstage behind the illusion of the theater. Putting his lesson to work, young Krull pretends to be sick so that he may stay home from school:

> I had produced these symptoms as effectively as though I had nothing to do with their appearance. I had improved upon nature, realized a dream; and only he who has succeeded in creating a compelling and effective reality out of nothing, out of sheer inward knowledge and contemplation—in short out of nothing more than imagination and the daring exploitation of his own body—he alone understands the strange and dreamlike satisfaction with which I rested from my creative task. (P. 36)

Both/And: Nature and Illusion in the Romances

Even now he further combines the roles of artist and thief, satisfying the hunger to which a solicitous physician has condemned him by eating stolen chocolates. But under the tutelage of another kind of teacher he learns his true role in Greek mythology. Having stolen a jewel case from a wealthy traveler at the customs office on the French border, Krull meets her again in his tenure as elevator boy at the Hotel St. James and Albany in Paris where, calling himself Armand, he becomes her lover:

> "You call me 'dear child'?" she cried, embracing me stormily and burying her mouth in my neck. "Oh, that's delicious! That's much better than 'sweet whore'! That's a much deeper delight than anything you've done, you artist in love. A little naked liftboy lies beside me, and calls me 'dear child,' me, Diane Philibert! *C'est exquis, ça me transporte! Armand, chéri,* I didn't mean to offend you. I didn't mean to say that you're especially stupid. All beauty is stupid because it simply exists as an object for glorification by the spirit. Let me see you, see you completely—heaven help me, how beautiful you are! The breast so sweet in its smooth, clear strength, the slim arms, the noble ribs, and narrow hips, and, oh, the Hermes legs—"
> "Stop it, Diane, this isn't right. It is I who should be praising you."
> "Nonsense! That's just a male convention. We women are lucky that our curves please you. But the divine, the masterpiece of creation, the model of beauty, that's you, you young, very young men with Hermes legs. Do you know who Hermes is?"
> "I must admit at the moment—"
> "*Celeste!* Diane Philibert is making love with someone who has never heard of Hermes! What a delicious degradation of the spirit! I will tell you, sweet fool, who Hermes is. He is the suave god of thieves." (P. 175)

Only now does Krull confess the theft of her jewelry, and her response caps one of the novel's funniest scenes. The soldier of fortune playing elevator boy must now devote his artistry to the role of thief in the acting out of Diane's favorite fantasy: while she pretends to lie asleep, he must steal her jewelry.

Like Autolycus, Krull combines Hermes' two roles in one, that of the confidence man, who uses his powers of transformation to turn his audiences into his victims. Thus, in his preinduction physical examination Krull plays the role of an eager would-be soldier afflicted by epilepsy. Like the artist that he is, he creates an illusion so potent that his medical audience, their interest kindled by the performance, must interpret every detail as a clue to a meaning which they can elucidate with critical superiority. For the confidence man, artistry is heroism; the creative ego asserts its force, whether in loving or in stealing, by transforming nature. The artist assumes his roles both to participate in life and to master it.

Autolycus's amoral mastery, we remember, adorns the fertility rites of *The Winter's Tale,* and the complexity of Shakespeare's vision refuses to allow us to separate the rogue from other aspects of art with which the play is concerned. Consider one sequence. Pretending to have been beaten and robbed so that he can pick the Clown's pocket, Autolycus announces that he will follow his victim to the festivities where he will add a new meaning to sheep-shearing by fleecing the shearers. As he leaves the stage singing an innocent ballad about the merry heart (most of his ballads are about transformation), the action moves to the ceremony. There immediately Florizel quiets Perdita's uneasiness about the propriety of playing the role of queen of the festival by observing that the gods themselves transform themselves, taking on human shapes. Now Perdita, the princess cast by life in the role of shepherdess, plays the queen of curds and cream while Polixenes suddenly assumes the frightening role Leontes

Both/And: Nature and Illusion in the Romances

had played in the comedy's tragic half. As she describes the
herbs and flowers she hands round, they become natural
symbols of the life represented in the play—of life renewed in the winter, of grace and remembrance—as if they
were nature's own art; and when Perdita rejects hybrid
flowers because art has abetted nature in producing them,
Polixenes replies conclusively that the art that mends nature is itself the product of nature. Or, as Autolycus puts it
in another key, "Sure the gods do this year connive at us,
and we may do anything extempore" (IV.iv.676–67).

That is Mann's point. The sheep-shearing of *The Confessions of Felix Krull* is the sequence in which the hero,
disguised as the Marquis de Venosta, listens with fascination to Professor Kuckuck's discourse on life in the dining
car of a train bound for Lisbon, and then, arrived at Lisbon,
visits the Professor's Museum of Natural History. Like
Prospero's island the museum is an image of both art and
nature, and there Krull comes to terms with the underlying paradox of the novel: man, occupant of a tiny corner of
space and time, is yet the grand climax of all nature's designs, and Krull, confidence man and player of roles, is
nature's end, its final product:

> All this inspired in me the moving reflection that
> these first beginnings, however absurd and lacking in
> dignity and usefulness, were preliminary moves in the
> direction of me—that is, of Man; and this it was that
> prompted my attitude of courteous self-possession as
> I was introduced to a marine saurian, a bare-skinned,
> sharp-jawed creature, represented by a five-metre-
> long model floating in a glass tank. (P. 301)

The comic equation demonstrated in the ensuing episodes
is that the force that created the universe and put it into
motion in time, into perpetual metamorphosis, is identical
to the force that moves Krull to the creation of his artistic
hegemony, his seduction of Zouzou Kuckuck, and his joyous account of his own exploits.

Both/And: Nature and Illusion in the Romances

What makes that account comic is what in other kinds if literature produces exactly the opposite effect: the centrality of ego in art and nature. That perception produces the ultimate irony of the *Confessions:* the hero who is artist of his own life is also the narrator, the artist who turns the materials of his own experience into the art that we experience. Only such a confidence man's trick can permit Mann to convey the almost inexpressible vision that controls the novel, in which life itself comes to seem like a work of art. Mann shares his vision with the Shakespeare of the romances, and it should thus be no surprise that in them Shakespeare takes pains to remind us that what we are watching is both life and art, reality and dream. Nor should we any longer be embarrassed by the autobiographical implications of Prospero. For Shakespeare's point in creating a protagonist who is both playwright and player and in unmistakably reminding us of his own career is not to make the audience think of him, but rather to make it see that the artist is himself the most potent image of the human condition as these works have been portraying it. The audience of such art should find it difficult to separate out its strands, to think of either nature or art apart from the other term. The simultaneity of the two paradigms, which seem to point at once in the opposite directions of nature and illusion, requires that we experience self-exploding nonsense as truth, the substantial world in which we live as fiction. To say only this about these inexhaustible plays and novels is surely in itself to be reductive.[18] But it is also to insist on a way of experiencing them that is less reductive than the one offered by some of the best criticism available. It insists, as such criticism does not, that art must be responded to as art. It reiterates with new force the truism that the translation of works of art into reasonable formulation betrays their essential nature.

Shakespeare's caprices on the relations between art and life, as I have argued elsewhere, only carry to its conclusion in his last phase a concern that is evident even in early works like *The Taming of the Shrew* and *A Midsummer Night's Dream*.[19] Similarly, in *The Holy Sinner* and *The Confessions of Felix Krull* Mann recapitulates and develops a nexus that, as is widely recognized, fascinated him throughout his entire career. In connection with the particular strategies of the two novels just discussed, it might be worth calling attention to the repeated motif in the *Joseph* series of the story as only a story, yet a story ordained by God, so that Laban, for example, acts as he does because he is playing a role.[20] Joseph stages the reunion with his family as an entertainment for God: "All that is Egyptian go out from me. . . . I invited God and the world to this play, but now shall God alone be witness" (p. 1114); and he summarizes his life as "only a play and a pattern" (p. 1207). The end of the gigantic story (p. 1207) is a kind of symbolic transformation of its events into a novel composed on one level by God, on another by Mann:

> Thus he spoke to them, and they laughed and wept together and stretched out their hands as he stood among them and touched him, and he too caressed them with his hands. And so endeth the beautiful story and God-invention [*die schöne Geschichte und Gotteserfindung*] of
> JOSEPH AND HIS BROTHERS.

This almost magical metamorphosis of the final tableau into the title of the novel plays on the ineffable permeability of the barrier between art and life as do the quickening of Hermione's statue at the end of *The Winter's Tale* and Prospero's epilogue, so trickily in and out of character, to *The Tempest*.

3

Mann contemplated the human condition once again in his final work, *Die Betrogene* (1953), Englished in 1954 as *The Black Swan*. Once again his fiction proves an uncanny

analogue to Shakespeare's final plays. Like them, it is retrospective, consciously allusive to the author's earlier
work, a virtual cadenza on the materials and themes of a
lifetime's art. A widow of fifty years falls shamelessly in
love with a boy, miraculously—as she thinks—resumes the
menstruation she has just left behind, casts decorum aside,
begins to rouge her cheeks and dress like a young woman.
At the height of her fever, having declared her love, she is
discovered to be in an advanced state of a cancer that is
responsible for her passion, her fever, her renewed excitement in life, her deceptive resumption of menstruation, and at the last her death. That Rosalie, married for
twenty years to a respectable military officer with whom
she lived in an industrial city, is a passionate romantic
deeply moved by nature, while her daughter Anna is a cold
and intellectual artist, is an almost tongue-in-cheek reversal of Mann's lifelong role assignments for bürgers and
artists, parents and children. Rosalie's late-blooming passion for an athletic, inscrutable, and beautiful young man
reenacts Aschenbach's love for Tadzio, and like it is inseparable from the disease that overwhelms her. The decaying rococo castle on the Rhine in a secret chamber of
which Rosalie, having maneuvered her Ken away from the
crowd of tourists with whom they are bound, avows her
love, "smells of death"[21] and is adorned with the exuber-
ant art of a sensual and self-indulgent culture; it is reached
by water, and fountains plash in its gardens: in a word, it is
the Venice of Aschenbach's death. As in *The Magic
Mountain* Rosalie and her daughter, representing consistently opposed positions, debate the questions of nature
vs. art, art vs. life, health vs. sickness, spiritual vs. material
causes of the inner life. Rosalie's dual motivation, in passion and in disease, recalls Leverkühn's in *Doctor Faustus,*
and as in that novel a third explanation is offered for
the outpouring of her soul: the work of the devil. For as
Rosalie, her daughter, and her beloved approach the castle, Rosalie, nibbling on a bit of stale bread intended for

the swans, incurs the resentment of the ominous black
swan who gives the novella its name and is not heard from
again, and Anna warns her jokingly "that the old devil
won't soon forget your robbing him of his food" (p. 124).

If the playful mastery of this story recalls Shakespeare's
last plays in its constantly ironic recall of its author's canon,
Mann's underlying concern with death and rebirth, with
the love of a nature that destroys as it creates, with the
mysteriousness of life and death, with the life-giving and
life-destroying powers of emotion, and his bittersweet
combination of compassion and detachment, do so even
more. Curiously , as in the sheep-shearing episode of *The
Winter's Tale,* so in *The Black Swan* the seasonality of
flowers is an issue crucial to one's understanding of all.
Early in the story Rosalie is horrified, then amused, to
discover that a haunting fragrance she encounters on a
walk with Anna is the "evil effluvium" of a nasty mound of
decaying excrement swarming with blowflies (pp. 22–24).
Later, rejoicing in the miracle of her renewed sexuality,
Rosalie delights in the resemblance of the earliest Febru-
ary flowers to the last blooms of autumn.

> "Isn't it remarkable," said Frau von Tümmler to her
> daughter, "how much they resemble the autumn col-
> chicum? It's practically the same flower! End and
> beginning—one could mistake them for each other,
> they are so alike—one could think one was back in
> autumn in the presence of a crocus, and believe in
> spring when one saw the last flower of the year."
> "Yes, a slight confusion," answered Anna. "Your
> old friend Mother Nature has a charming propensity
> for the equivocal and for mystification in general."
> (pp. 109–10)

Perdita's anxiety about the equivocal flowers, grown
"Not yet on summer's death nor on the birth / Of trem-
bling winter," centers on the art-nature issue that, as we
have seen, bears on much of *The Winter's Tale,* but it

Both/And: Nature and Illusion in the Romances

allows Shakespeare to make a similar point about the proximity of spring to winter, life to death. In ravishing lines she wishes for spring flowers "To make you garlands of; and my sweet friend, to strew him o'er and o'er!" "What, like a corpse?" exclaims Florizel, and she answers,

> No, like a bank, for love to lie and play on:
> Not like a corpse; or if—not to be buried,
> But quick, and in mine arms. (IV.iv.128–32)

The rebirth enacted and celebrated in the sheepshearing anticipates the reawakening of Hermione and of Leontes' marriage to her after their sixteen years of winter, and as the reconciliations come about so that young lovers and old parents may resume their natural roles, the loyal Paulina, her work done, recalls the truth of death awaiting the vanguard of the joyous procession:

> I, an old turtle,
> Will wing me to some withered bough, and there
> My mate (that's never to be found again)
> Lament, till I am lost. (V.iii.132–35)

If the conventions of a miracle turned back into mere comedy require that instead she marry Camillo and join in the festivities, the point has been made nonetheless: death is as real in the life of this play as it is intrusive into its genre, and life and death alike are to be celebrated as processes inextricably intertwined. Paulina's withered bough touches Perdita's pastoral summer with winter's death.

The heroine of Mann's last romance dies with an explicit understanding of the mystery on her lips:

> "Anna, never say that Nature deceived me, that she is sardonic and cruel. Do not rail at her, as I do not. I am loth to go away—from you all, from life with its spring. But how should there be spring without death? Indeed, death is a great instrument of life,

and if for me it borrowed the guise of resurrection, of the joy of love, that was not a lie, but goodness and mercy."

Another little push, closer to her daughter, and a failing whisper:

"Nature—I have always loved her, and she—has been loving to her child." (Pp. 140–41)

The explicit and insistent thematizing of *The Black Swan* differentiates it from the more implicit and authentic art of the last great novels, making it a parable in the style of some of Mann's earliest works. But the theme itself is a paradox so unresolvable that only the charm of his story-telling can make it plausible. And that very paradox, as we have seen, is at the center of Shakespeare's late work. It can be explicated, and it would be dishonest to pretend that I have not been trying to explicate it. But what disappears in the explication is the experience itself. Even in describing Mann's novella thematically one necessarily omits the combination of a nagging sense of mortification with elation and compassion that Rosalie Tümmler's state evokes, a state simultaneously touching, grotesque, comic, disgusting, frightening, and admirable. For it is that multiple experience, created by the discipline and delicacy of his art, which Mann strives to arouse in us. The experience of his art, then, is akin to the experience of life, as the dying artist sees it, in all its contradictory yet ultimately harmonious multiplicity. The thematic reduction explicit in Rosalie's last speeches no more expresses the life of his novella than her perception can be said to explain the meaning of life.

And Mann almost tells us as much: for the bald thematic assertion of the ending is set against a backdrop that reminds us with unceasing playfulness, as I have suggested, that this story is a self-conscious parody of some of Mann's major works. On the one hand, then, art that insists on its artifice; on the other, homiletic thematizing that insists on its abstractness; and in the end, despite all, the confidence trick of achieved art. We see the novelist pull the ropes, but hear the bells ring of their own accord.

If Shakespeare reminds us in his last plays of the Renaissance commonplace that the artist is a second God creating a second nature, he does so in order to share a more profound perception that God has created our universe as a work of art. Seen from the point of view common to the romances we have considered, art and life are one. "Your actions are my dreams,"[22] says Leontes to Hermione in a profoundly ironic moment—ironic because on one level of our awareness his jealousy is only a matter of his dreams, on another because so much in the play is called dream at one point or another that all its objective reality comes to seem like a dream to its participants, and finally because the play itself is our dream of wish-fulfillment, a transformation of the art of tragedy into the life of comedy. "What is called fate," Felix Krull observes, "is actually ourselves, working through unknown but infallible laws" (p. 119). Subject and object merge in the self seen as a player of roles in a plot whose outcome and meaning are determined by a coalition between ego and providence that leads always to poetic justice. If such justice requires that we be aware of moral law, the moral implications of the hero's actions ultimately matter less than their quality as spectacle. Every motion of the spirit, every event of life, is infinitely serious, yet, as such stuff as dreams are made on, as an inconsequential ripple on the flux of time, infinitely trivial, the subject of an entertainment for a play's audience constantly reminded it is an audience, and for the gods.

4

In the troubled and troubling plays of Shakespeare's earlier years the kind of artistic multivalence for which I have been arguing is the mirror of an unfathomable reality which is the source of the trouble. *The Merchant of Venice* undercuts or at least suggests the impractability of the very paradigm it leads its audiences to desire, positing as necessary a charity which seems uncharitable in its operation and hinting a similar paradox in the operation of the universe. In *Henry V* the world is presented as equally reducible to opposite paradigms, each equally compelling, only one of which can be chosen. Responding to the play's urgent duality, we are tempted to sense in its creator a crisis of understanding and belief comparable to the one he induces in us. In the tragedies we examined, disturbing mysteries lie beyond the understanding to which they drive us, and we are repeatedly led to locate the essence of tragedy precisely there, in the inadequacy of reasonable understanding. Each of the plays we have considered thus dramatizes, in its own way, the limitations of thematizing.

In the last plays, however, we see a different phenomenon. Shakespeare does not ask us to reject a pattern to which a play seems reducible: he asks us to accept an overlay of patterns, paradoxically embracing the contradictory gestalts of nature and art. My study has not been biographical, but its conclusions add support from a new point of view for the generally established opinion that the romances reflect a new kind of acceptance and peace in Shakespeare as he drew his work to a close, an ability to live at ease with the intransigent reality that is the cause in his earlier work of tragic intensity. The very quality of his artist's view of the world that made his earlier plays so often disturbing, the recognition of a reality that cannot be cut down to a single understanding, is the source of much of the energy of his final plays.

Notes

Chapter 1

1. For hostile accounts of these and other attacks on the old consensus, see M. H. Abrams, "How to Do Things with Texts," *Partisan Review* 46 (1979), 566–588, and Gerald Graff, *Literature against Itself: Literary Ideas in Modern Society* (Chicago: University of Chicago Press, 1979).

2. Richard Levin, *New Readings vs. Old Plays: Recent Trends in the Reinterpretation of English Renaissance Drama* (Chicago: University of Chicago Press, 1979).

3. Ibid., p. ix.

4. Ibid., pp. 2–5; italics his.

5. Ibid., p. 10.

6. Ibid., pp 7–8.

7. Ibid., p. 202.

8. For a useful survey of the theatrical vicissitudes of Shylock, see Toby Lelyveld, *Shylock on the Stage* (Cleveland: Press of Western Reserve University, 1961).

9. Paul N. Siegel, *Shakespeare in His Time and Ours* (Notre Dame: University of Notre Dame Press, 1968), p. 245.

10. John W. Draper, "The Theme of *The Merchant of Venice*," *Stratford to Dogberry: Studies in Shakespeare's Earlier Plays* (Pittsburgh: University of Pittsburgh Press, 1961), p. 128.

11. Harold C. Goddard, *The Meaning of Shakespeare* (Chicago: University of Chicago Press, 1960; 1st ed. 1951), I, 85. In view of the argument to be developed here and of my general admiration of Goddard, it should be noted that the title of his posthumous book was assigned by the publisher.

12. H. B. Charlton, *Shakespearian Comedy* (London: Macmillan, 1966; 1st ed. 1938), p. 159.

13. Norman Nathan, "Three Notes on *The Merchant of Venice*," *Shakespeare Association Bulletin* 23 (1948), p. 155.

14. The latter interpretation is Goddard's.

15. On legal matters in the play see John Palmer, *Comic Characters of Shakespeare* (London: Macmillan, 1946), pp. 64–65, and George W. Keeton, *Shakespeare and His Legal Problems* (London: A. C. Black, 1930), pp. 10–21.

16. My text for all Shakespeare citations unless otherwise specified is *The Riverside Shakespeare*, ed. G. B. Evans et al. (Boston: Houghton Mifflin, 1974).

17. L. Teeter, "Scholarship and the Art of Criticism," *ELH* 5 (1938), 187, accurately sums up the conflict: "There is little doubt that Shakespeare, consciously at least, intended this passage to raise a laugh at the expense of Shylock. Yet to many cultured readers of today it is to a large extent a pathetic speech arousing a sympathetic pity for the mistreated father." C. L. Barber, *Shakespeare's Festive Comedy* (Cleveland and New York: Meridian Books, 1963; 1st ed. 1959), p. 184, argues that at the end of this scene "there *is* pathos; but it is being fed into the comic mill and makes the laughter all the more hilarious."

18. Thus H. B. Charlton, *Shakespearian Comedy*, p. 160, asserts: "However one reads the play, it is certain that the intentions of the author were in many ways defeated. Shylock, Antonio, Portia and Jessica do not stand forth as they were meant to do. The parts they were called upon to play by their author's prejudices did not square with those the dramatist worked out for them. There is throughout the clash of rival schemes, the proposals of Shakespeare's deliberate will, and the disposals of his creative imagination."

19. E. E. Stoll, *Shakespearian Studies: Historical and Comparative in Method* (New York: Macmillan, 1927), pp. 255–366.

20. See for example S. C. Sen Gupta, *Shakespearian Comedy* (Oxford: Oxford University Press, 1950), p. 132, and John Middleton Murry, *Shakespeare* (London: J. Cape, 1936), pp. 194, 199.

21. Lawrence W. Hyman, "The Rival Lovers in *The Merchant of Venice*," *SQ* 21 (1970), 109; see also Peter G. Phialas, *Shakespeare's Romantic Comedies: The Development of Their Form and*

Meaning (Chapel Hill: University of North Carolina Press, 1966), p. 135, where virtually the same statement is made.

22. Hyman, "The Rival Lovers, " p. 110.

23. A few instances will suffice. Draper, "The Theme of *The Merchant of Venice*," p. 135: "Shylock the Jew was merely Venetian local color; Shylock the usurer was a commentary on London life." Bernard Grebanier, *The Truth about Shylock* (New York: Random House, 1962), p. x: "Shylock is not only a Jew, he is also a prototype of the banker," and Shakespeare's real interest is in attacking the impersonality of banks. Siegel, *Shakespeare in His Time and Ours,* p. 245, justifies audience hatred of Shylock on the grounds that Shakespeare was after Puritans rather than Jews. Thomas H. Fujimura, "Mode and Structure in *The Merchant of Venice*," *PMLA* 81 (1966), 504, writes: "The most serious obstacle to grasping the ironic mode in which he is presented is to regard Shylock primarily as a Jew. In adapting the bond story, Shakespeare stressed his Jewish traits, no doubt for the practical reason that the associations worked to communicate the theme with the greatest economy on the Elizabethan stage. But he is hateful not because he is a Jew but because he is Shylock...Jessica...is ashamed not of her father's Jewishness but of his 'manners,' that is, his character. Shylock's Jewishness is thus, in Aristotelian terms, an 'accident'; his substance is his spiritual deadness or leadenness."

24. Fujimura, "Mode and Structure," p. 501.

25. A notable example of this sort of reductiveness is the account by Phialas (n. 21 above), where the literal meaning of the plot is traded in for a symbolic reading which, when it cannot be demonstrated fully to dominate the play, is patronized as a relatively primitive attempt by Shakespeare (though far advanced beyond the earlier plays) to dispose of some themes the dramatist had been working out. See especially pp. 153, 168–69.

26. Frank Kermode, "The Mature Comedies," in John Russell Brown and Bernard Harris, eds., *Early Shakespeare,* Stratford-upon-Avon Studies, 3, (New York: Capricorn Books, 1966; 1st ed. 1961), p. 224.

27. Brown, introduction to his New Arden edition of *The Merchant of Venice* (London: Methuen, 1959; 1st ed. 1955); "The Realization of Shylock: a Theatrical Criticism," in *Early Shakespeare,* pp. 187–210; "Love's Wealth and the Judgement of *The*

Merchant of Venice," *Shakespeare and His Comedies* (London: Methuen, 1962; 1st ed. 1957), pp. 45–81; Barber, *Shakespeare's Festive Comedy*, pp. 162–91; Palmer, *Comic Characters of Shakespeare;* Danson, *The Harmonies of The Merchant of Venice* (New Haven: Yale University Press, 1978). Despite his eccentrically systematized reading, Fujimura interprets the play similarly, as does Grebanier. John S. Coolidge, "Law and Love in *The Merchant of Venice*," *SQ* 27 (1976), 243–63, is less compelling critically but more firmly grounded theologically than other critics. See also John S. Weld, *Meaning in Comedy* (Albany: State University of New York Press, 1975), pp. 207–37.

28. Barber, *Shakespeare's Festive Comedy*, p. 170.

29. Brown, Introduction to Arden edition, p. lviii.

30. John R. Cooper, "Shylock's Humanity," *SQ* 21 (1970), 117–24.

31. Ibid., p. 123.

32. Palmer, *Comic Characters*, p. 86.

33. Barber, *Shakespeare's Festive Comedy*, pp. 170, 189.

34. Brown, Introduction to Arden edition, p. lviii.

35. Brown, *Shakespeare and His Comedies*, p. 74.

36. Barber, *Shakespeare's Festive Comedy*, p. 4.

37. Cooper, "Shylock's Humanity," p. 121.

38. Stanley Cavell, *Must We Mean What We Say?* (New York: Charles Scribner's Sons, 1969), pp. 236–37.

39. Writing from his orthodox point of view, Coolidge remarks: "The question is often asked whether there can be such a thing as Christian tragedy; this play seems to ask whether there can be such a thing as Christian comedy. Shakespeare answers in the affirmative, relying on the great biblical principle by which the old creation both points toward and rejects the new, while the new both abolishes and fulfills the old" (p. 260).

40. Sigurd Burckhardt, *Shakespearean Meanings* (Princeton: Princeton University Press, 1968), p. 224.

41. Brown, *Shakespeare and His Comedies*, p. 70.

42. Though Richards, Empson, et al., succeeded in establishing the invalidity of simple meanings consistent with one statement quoted from a literary context, and Richards in his *Philosophy of Rhetoric* argued for a "context" theory of meaning, the fruit of their labor has been a more deft exploration of more complex and inclusive meanings which ultimately leads to para-

phrase. Looked at from the vantage point of the present day, Cleanth Brooks's *The Well Wrought Urn* (New York: Reynal and Hitchcock, 1947) seems less free from an overriding concern with meaning and paraphrase than it did in 1947. Though some of his argument in "The Heresy of Paraphrase" (*The Well Wrought Urn,* pp. 176–96) would seem almost to have stated my case for me, Brooks finally absorbs much of the traditional position he is attacking in his insistence on a "real core of meaning which constitutes the essence of the poem." "Structure," which Brooks proposes as an alternative to Winters's "rational meaning," leads equally to hypostasis because it is not finally concerned with the interaction between signal and response, focusing rather on "the unification of attitudes into a hierarchy subordinated to a total and governing attitude" within the poem (p. 189).

43. E. D. Hirsch, Jr., *Validity in Interpretation* (New Haven: Yale University Press, 1967), p. 22.

44. Levin, *New Readings vs. Old Plays,* p. 29. On the fallacy of building interpretations by the accretion of simpler previous readings, see Hirsch, *Validity in Interpretation,* p. 230. As Hirsch points out, "the most inclusive interpretation," in all probability, necessarily ignores the crucial matter of emphasis.

45. *Poems in Persons: An Introduction to the Psychoanalysis of Literature* (New York: W. W. Norton, 1973) and *Five Readers Reading* (New Haven: Yale University Press, 1975).

46. Here Hirsch's distinction between "meaning" and "significance" is useful.

47. Hirsch, *Validity in Interpretation,* p. 126.

48. Hyder Rollins, ed., *The Letters of John Keats, 1814–1821* (Cambridge: Harvard University Press, 1958), I, 193.

49. Kenneth Burke, *The Philosophy of Literary Form* (New York: Vintage Books, 1957), pp. viii, 9; italics his.

50. René Wellek, *Theory of Literature,* new rev. ed. (New York: Harvest Books, 1956), p. 156.

51. See especially *Emotion and Meaning in Music* (Chicago: University of Chicago Press, 1956) and *Music, the Arts, and Ideas: Patterns and Predictions in Twentieth-Century Culture* (Chicago: University of Chicago Press, 1967).

52. Maynard Mack, "The Jacobean Shakespeare: Some Observations on the Construction of the Tragedies," in John Russell Brown and Bernard Harris, eds., *Jacobean Theatre,*

Stratford-upon-Avon Studies, I (London: Edward Arnold, 1960); Stephen Booth, "On the Value of *Hamlet,*" in Norman Rabkin, ed., *Reinterpretations of Elizabethan Drama* (New York: Columbia University Press, 1969), pp. 137–76, and Booth's *Shakespeare's Sonnets,* edited with analytic commentary (New Haven: Yale University Press, 1977), p. x.; E. A. J. Honigmann, "Shakespearian Tragedy and the Mixed Response," An Inaugural Lecture (University of Newcastle upon Tyne, 1971), pp. 25, 24; Michael Goldman, *Shakespeare and the Energies of Drama* (Princeton: Princeton University Press, 1972); John Russell Brown, "Theatrical Research and the Criticism of Shakespeare and His Contemporaries," *SQ* 13 (1962), 451–61, "The Theatrical Element of Shakespeare Criticism," in Rabkin, *Reinterpretations of Elizabethan Drama,* and *Free Shakespeare* (London: Heineman, 1974); Marvin Rosenberg, *The Masks of Othello, The Masks of King Lear, The Masks of Macbeth* (Berkeley and Los Angeles: University of California Press, 1971, 1972, 1978); Susan Snyder, *The Comic Matrix of Shakespeare's Tragedies* (Princeton: Princeton University Press, 1979); for book-length studies by the psychoanalytic critics named, see Coppélia Kahn, *Man's Estate: Masculine Identity in Shakespeare* (Berkeley and Los Angeles: University of California Press, 1980), Meredith A. Skura, *The Critic and the Psychoanalyst: Literary Uses of the Psychoanalytic Process* (New Haven: Yale University Press, 1980), and Richard P. Wheeler, *Shakespeare's Development and the Problem Comedies: Turn and Counterturn* (Berkeley and Los Angeles: University of California Press, 1980); see also Coppélia Kahn and Murray Schwartz, eds., *Representing Shakespeare: New Psychoanalytic Essays* (Baltimore: Johns Hopkins University Press, 1980).

53. Immanuel Kant, preface to the first edition, *Critique of Pure Reason,* tr. Norman Kemp Smith (London: Macmillan, 1934), p. 5.

54. Graff, *Literature against Itself,* p. 143.

55. Ibid., p. 144.

Chapter 2

1. Karl P. Wentersdorf, "The Conspiracy of Silence in *Henry V,*" *SQ* 27 (1976), p. 265. See Wentersdorf's nn. 3 and 4 for

representatives of both points of view. Though inconclusive itself, Wentersdorf's essay presents evidence apparently intended to suggest that the truth lies somewhere between, a position to be discussed below. Another useful survey of the controversy will be found in Gordon Ross Smith, "Shakespeare's *Henry V: Another Part of the Critical Forest," JHI* 37 (1976), 3–26.

2. E. H. Gombrich, *Art and Illusion: A Study of the Psychology of Pictorial Representation* (New York: Pantheon Books, 1960), pp. 5–6.

3. Sherman H. Hawkins astutely describes Prince John in "Virtue and Kingship in Shakespeare's *Henry IV," ELR* 5 (1975), 335–36.

4. A. R. Humphreys, ed., *The Second Part of King Henry IV,* The Arden Shakespeare (London: Methuen, 1966), p. 176.

5. See Jonas A. Barish, "The Turning Away of Prince Hal," *Shakespeare Studies,* I (1965), 9–17.

6. J. Dover Wilson, *The Fortunes of Falstaff* (Cambridge: Cambridge University Press, 1943).

7. Harold C. Goddard, *The Meaning of Shakespeare* (Chicago: University of Chicago Press, 1951), I, 266.

8. Whether or not the King is hypocritical, as Goddard claims, in crediting his victory to God, this is certainly one reason for the assertion.

9. Hawkins, "Virtue and Kingship," pp. 313–20, and passim.

10. Goldman, *Shakespeare and the Energies of Drama,* p. 70.

11. Hotspur's touching relationship with *his* Kate in *1 Henry IV* is one of the few qualities suggesting his superiority to Hal that are not proved illusory by the end of that play. In the ease and affection of his partnership with a woman smart and brassy enough to recall still another Kate, Petruchio's bride, Hotspur shows a sexual integration we don't see in his cousin until the end of *Henry V.*

12. Norman Rabkin, *Shakespeare and the Common Understanding* (New York: The Free Press, 1967), pp. 98–110.

13. Levin, *New Readings vs. Old Plays,* pp. 108–10, rejects critical suggestions that these lines are intended to cast a shadow on the celebratory ending: "In *Henry V,* to be sure, there is one lonely piece of internal evidence—a single line in the Epilogue [*sic*]— which does point to those future disasters, and which has therefore been seized upon by all of these critics who wish us to see

beyond the ending. But the context here makes it perfectly clear that the disasters are not to be blamed upon Henry (unless he can be blamed for dying too soon), and in no way diminish his 'glory.' . . . If he had really intended to project the ending of this play onto 'the grim path from Agincourt to Tewksbury,' Shakespeare (or any playwright of the most minimal competence) could surely have done much better than that." Levin's insistence that we take the happy ending fully at face value fails to account for the fact that Shakespeare unnecessarily appends these lines to the play, as it fails equally to notice the negative context into which pessimistic predictions fit naturally. And "blame" is not the issue.

14. Arthur Sherbo, ed., *Johnson on Shakespeare*. Yale Edition of the Works of Samuel Johnson (New Haven: Yale University Press, 1966), VIII, 552.

15. Goddard, *The Meaning of Shakespeare* (I, 219–21) brilliantly analyzes the speech to show how it undercuts Henry's claim to his own throne in England as well.

16. J. H. Walter, *King Henry V*, The Arden Shakespeare (London: Methuen, 1954), p. xxv.

17. A. C. Bradley, "The Rejection of Falstaff," *Oxford Lectures on Poetry*, 2d. ed. (London: Macmillan, 1909), p. 257. Hawkins, "Virtue and Kingship" (p. 341), sees Henry as "the true inheritor of Edward the Black Prince," the genealogy as "not ironic," and "Henry's right to France . . . vindicated by a higher power than Canterbury."

18. Walter, *Henry V*, p. xxv; sic.

19. Goddard, *The Meaning of Shakespeare*, I, 215–68.

20. Ibid., p. 256.

21. Hawkins, "Virtue and Kingship," p. 340.

22. Ibid., p. 341.

23. Sherbo, *Johnson on Shakespeare*, p. 566.

24. Ibid., p. 563.

25. Ibid., p. 346.

26. Hawkins, "Virtue and Kingship," p. 321.

27. Goddard, *The Meaning of Shakespeare*, I, 267.

28. Ibid., p. 260.

29. Una Ellis-Fermor, "Shakespeare's Political Plays," *The Frontiers of Drama* (London: Methuen, 1945).

30. Sherbo, *Johnson on Shakespeare*, p. 556.

31. A. P. Rossiter, "Ambivalence—The Dialectic of the Histories," *Angel with Horns* (New York: Theatre Art Books, 1961).

32. See, for a sensitive example, Robert Ornstein, *A Kingdom for a Stage: The Achievement of Shakespeare's History Plays* (Cambridge: Harvard University Press, 1972). Gordon Ross Smith (see n. 1, above) takes a sophisticated version of the middle position, ably demonstrating the evidence for positive and negative views and concluding that they both demand recognition: "Shakespeare has accepted [Henry V's] surface reputation without relinquishing the sordid details that brought the heroic action into being" (p. 26).

33. William Empson, *Seven Types of Ambiguity* (New York: Meridian, 1955; first published 1947), p. 217.

34. See, for example, Michael McCanles, *Dialectical Criticism and Renaissance Literature* (Berkeley and Los Angeles: University of California Press, 1975), Bernard McElroy, *Shakespeare's Mature Tragedies* (Princeton: Princeton University Press, 1973), Marion B. Smith, *Dualities in Shakespeare* (Toronto: University Press, 1966), Janet Adelman, *The Common Liar: An Essay on Antony and Cleopatra* (New Haven: Yale University Press, 1973), and Robert Grudin, *Mighty Opposites: Shakespeare and Renaissance Contrariety* (Berkeley and Los Angeles: University of California Press, 1979).

35. Rabkin, *Shakespeare and the Common Understanding,* pp. 20–26.

Chapter 3

1. John Dryden, *All for Love,* V.509–19, in *John Dryden: Four Tragedies,* ed. L. A. Beaurline and Fredson Bowers (Chicago: University of Chicago Press, 1967).

2. See, for example, Antony's fine arias at I.292–311 and II.281–91.

3. For a full development of this view, see Arthur C. Kirsch, *Dryden's Heroic Drama* (Princeton: Princeton University Press, 1965), pp. 126ff.

4. R. J. Kaufmann, introduction to his edition of *All for Love* (San Francisco: Chandler Publishing Co., 1962), p. xvi. Kaufmann's brilliant essay is particularly valuable in its exploration of

the retrospective aspects of the play, but helpful also on the treatment of conflict.

5. Kirsch, *Dryden's Heroic Drama,* pp. 51ff., sees Dryden's emphasis on this conflict as influenced by Corneille.

6. For the best developed reading of *Antony and Cleopatra* in terms like this, see Janet Adelman, *The Common Liar.* For a discussion of complementarity, see my *Shakespeare and the Common Understanding,* particularly Chapter 1.

7. While conceding that neither alternative open to Antony is especially attractive, Beaurline and Bowers argue in the introduction to *Four Plays* that the play is more dialectical than I think it is, and that Antony makes "the right choices" (p. 20). Dryden's own insistence on the obligation of the dramatist to provide clear moral understanding is forthrightly stated in the *Preface to Troilus and Cressida, Containing the Grounds of Criticism in Tragedy,* written the year after *All for Love:* "'Tis the moral that directs the whole action of the play to one center; and that action or fable is the example built upon the moral, which confirms the truth of it to our experience: when the fable is designed, then and not before, the persons are to be introduced with their manners, characters, and passions." *Literary Criticism of John Dryden,* ed. Arthur C. Kirsch (Lincoln: University of Nebraska Press, 1966). For an unusually sensitive study of Dryden's rationalistic assumptions about tragedy, focused on *Troilus and Cressida,* see Tetsuo Kishi, "Dryden and Shakespeare," *Shakespeare Studies,* X, 1971–72 (Shakespeare Society of Japan, 1974), 39–51.

8. Eugene M. Waith, *The Herculean Hero* (London: Chatto and Windus, 1962), p. 200.

9. "Dryden . . . attempts to transport his reader or viewer to an intellectual Olympus from which the general tendencies and follies of mankind can be viewed. Society, in Dryden's view, contains many misguided individuals but few evil men. One finds no villains like Iago or Goneril in these plays: the tyrants, traitors, and rebels are all acting from a conviction of the rightness of their action; they may have begun with an erroneous premise (for instance, that chance rules all events or that power is divine), but then deduced their thoughts and actions accurately from that premise. By means of such characters, Dryden invites his audience to a tolerant appraisal of their fellowman; he

suggests that incorrect thinking, not wicked hearts, brings about rebellions or tyrannies. Underlying Dryden's dramatic technique is the optimistic idea that if men can be made to reason correctly their wills or desires will follow suit." Anne T. Barbeau, *The Intellectual Design of John Dryden's Heroic Plays* (New Haven: Yale University Press, 1970), p. 9.

10. E.g., IV.43–52.

11. Barbeau demonstrates convincingly how superficial are the apparent conflicts in the meanings of Dryden's plays, suggesting that as a sophisticated writer for a sophisticated audience he had to imply an intellectual tension that in fact his syllogistic playwriting precluded (*Dryden's Heroic Plays,* p. 17). The audience's assurance that there is a discoverable right side to the argument is, according to Robert B. Heilman, *Tragedy and Melodrama: Versions of Experience* (Seattle: University of Washington Press, 1968), the distinguishing mark of melodrama as opposed to tragedy.

12. *Dryden's Heroic Drama,* pp. 35ff.

13. *The Herculean Hero,* p. 201.

14. II.ii.34–35; my text is Thomas Otway, *Venice Preserved,* ed. Malcolm Kelsall (Lincoln: University of Nebraska Press, 1969).

15. Cf. his advice to Jaffeir when the latter laments Priuli's unkindness to Belvidera: "Burn! First burn, and level Venice to thy ruin!" (I.i.277–78).

16. The epithet "itching," I.i.187 for Antonio, III.ii.274, 454 for Renault.

17. The dagger which emblematizes Jaffeir's tragic isolation from both the factions he loves, paralleled by another dagger with which Aquilina wants Pierre to kill *her;* contiguous parallel scenes involving now Belvidera and Jaffeir, now Aquilina and Pierre; Aquilina beset by Shaftesbury-Antonio, ending one scene (III.i) with the lines, "Thus when godlike lover was displeased, / We sacrifice our fool and he's appeased," Belvidera beset by Shaftesbury-Renault opening the next with "I'm sacrificed! I am sold! betrayed to shame!"

18. IV.ii.5–10.

19. Final destruction seize on all the world!
  Bend down, ye Heavens, and shutting round this earth,
  Crush the vile globe in its first confusion;
  Scorch it with elemental flames to one cursed cinder,

> And all us little creepers in't, called men
> Burn, burn to nothing. . . . (V.ii.93–98)

20. Blasted be every herb and fruit and tree,
    Cursed be the rain that falls upon the earth,
    And may the general curse reach man and beast.

    .   .   .   .

    The air's too thin, and pierces my weak brain,
    I long for thick substantial sleep. (V.iii.225–34)

21. I.i.49–50.

22. I brought her, gave her to your despairing arms;
    Indeed you thanked me; but a nobler gratitude
    Rose in her soul; for from that hour she loved me,
    Till for her life she paid me with herself. (45–50)

23. E.g., III.ii.61–75, 113–16.

24. For succinct discussion of the historical sources, see Kelsall's introduction to *Venice Preserved,* xiv–xvii, though his reading of Otway's interpretation of the materials differs from mine.

25. II.iii.96–99, 132–34.

26. Perhaps more pointed than revelation of the covering up of private motive with the rhetoric of public interest among the conspirators is Antonio's reaction to the discovery in the Senate that the conspiracy has been formed at the house of his mistress Aquilina and to the order to search her house:

> What, my Nicky Nacky, hurry durry, Nicky in the plot—
> I'll make a speech. Most noble Senators,
> What headlong apprehension drives you on,
> Right noble, wise, and truly solid Senators,
> To violate the laws and right of nations. . . . (IV.ii.81–85)

27. Eugene M. Waith, *The Pattern of Tragicomedy in Beaumont and Fletcher* (New Haven: Yale University Press, 1952). See also Eric Rothstein *Restoration Tragedy: Form and the Process of Change* (Madison: University of Wisconsin Press, 1967), pp. 55–59, though I disagree with his contention that Fletcher is primarily concerned with the use of narrative technique. Waith's insights have been sensitively developed in a fine essay by Arthur C. Kirsch, *Jacobean Dramatic Perspectives* (Charlottesville: University Press of Virginia, 1972), pp. 38–51.

28. E.g., III.ii.341ff., when a noble, Caesar-like speech from the already discredited villain Renault prompts Jaffeir's "wonder at thy virtue."

29. Contrast her repudiation of rapine and destruction (IV.i.42ff.) with Renault's similarly phrased invitation to them (III.ii.373ff.).

30. For an account of Shakespeare's popularity in the period, see Rothstein, *Restoration Tragedy,* pp. 51–54.

31. My text of Tate's 1681 play is that of *Five Restoration Adaptations of Shakespeare,* ed. Christopher Spencer (Urbana: University of Illinois Press, 1965).

32. Stanley Cavell, "The Avoidance of Love: A Reading of *King Lear," Must We Mean What We Say?,* pp. 267–353; Marvin Rosenberg, *The Masks of King Lear,* p. 246 and passim. See also Janet Adelman, Introduction to *Twentieth-Century Interpretations of King Lear* (Englewood Cliffs: Prentice-Hall, 1978), pp. 1–21.

33. See, for example, Cavell and Rosenberg, cited in n. 32 above; Stephen Booth, "On the Greatness of *King Lear,"* in Adelman, *Interpretations of King Lear;* Maynard Mack, *King Lear in Our Time* (Berkeley and Los Angeles: University of California Press, 1965); Rosalie L. Colie and F. T. Flahiff, *Some Facets of King Lear: Essays in Prismatic Criticism* (Toronto: University of Toronto Press, 1974), where a dozen single perspectives simultaneously demonstrate in how many ways the play can responsibly be interpreted and how impossible it is to reduce the tragedy to what can be seen from any of them.

34. His weakness often takes the form of a sentimental notion of power based on a familial idea that has little to do with reality, as when, at his coronation, he assumes that since the squabbling Somerset and York are both his kinsmen he can safely appoint them joint commanders: "Both are my kinsmen and I love them both" (IV.i.155).

35. The classic study of the Renaissance analogy between the body and the body politic is Ernst H. Kantorowicz, *The King's Two Bodies* (Princeton: Princeton University Press, 1957). For a valuable recent study, see Leonard Barkan, *Nature's Work of Art: The Human Body as Image of the World* (New Haven: Yale University Press, 1975), particularly Chapter 2, "The Human Body and the Commonwealth."

36. Lawrence Stone, *The Family, Sex, and Marriage in England, 1500–1800* (New York: Harper and Row, 1977), pp. 123–50.

37. Edward I. Berry, *Patterns of Decay: Shakespeare's Early Histories* (Charlottesville: University Press of Virginia, 1975), p. 23. On the significance of family in the tetralogy, see Robert P. Pierce, *Shakespeare's History Plays: The Family and the State* (Columbus: Ohio State University Press, 1971), pp. 35–88, a sensitive essay that reaches some conclusions consonant with my own; see also Ronald Berman, "Fathers and Sons in the Henry VI Plays," *SQ* 13 (1962), 487–97.

38. David Riggs, *Shakespeare's Heroical Histories: Henry VI and Its Literary Tradition* (Cambridge: Harvard University Press, 1971), p. 109.

39. This understanding of the contrast between Talbot and Joan is greatly indebted to Rigg's study.

40. Freud's rather disappointing remarks on Richard III are to be found in "Some Character-Types Met with in Psycho-Analytic Work" (1916), *Standard Edition of the Complete Psychological Works of Sigmund Freud,* tr. James Strachey et al. (London: Hogarth Press, 1953–74), 14:313–15. Wolfgang Clemen, *Kommentar zu Shakespeares Richard III: Interpretation eines Dramas,* (Göttingen: Vandenhoeck and Ruprecht, 1957), pp. 20–22. In "History, Character and Conscience in *Richard III,*" *Comparative Drama* V (1971), 301–31, Richard P. Wheeler offers a valuable psychoanalytic study of Richard, more plausible in its identification of Richard's destructive and self-destructive psychology than in its attempt to prove that the character's problems arise from an unresolved infantile conflict. What is most convincing about Wheeler's demonstration is its recognition of psychological problems deeper than the moral wickedness of the surface—just what Cibber could not see.

41. It is striking that the critic who wants to prove that Richard is conventionally motivated by ambition must go to *3 Henry VI* for his primary evidence. There Shakespeare's earlier Richard is given such lines as "I'll make my heaven to dream upon the crown" (III.ii.168) and "Can I do this, and cannot get a crown?" (III.ii.194), though even in that speech he devotes far more energy to celebrating his ability to "add colors to the chameleon, / Change shapes with Proteus for advantages, / And set the murderous Machevil to school" (191–93) than to dreaming of the pleasures of kingship. My contention that Richard's real motivation in *Richard III* is the desire to destroy his family is just as subject to the charge that it is a reduction as

the more traditional explanation that I reject. It is clear, however, that Shakespeare seems to go out of his way in his last play
about Richard to avoid suggesting that he is motivated primarily
by ambition.

42. On the stage history of *Richard III,* see the essay by C. B.
Young in the New Cambridge Shakespeare, ed. J. Dover Wilson
(Cambridge: The University Press, 1954), pp. xlvi–lxi.

43. *The Tragical History of King Richard III. As it is now Acted
at the Theatre Royal in Drury Lane. Alter'd from Shakespear, by Mr.
Cibber,* in *Plays written by Mr. Cibber in Two Volumes* (London,
1721, the first edition). The play was first performed in 1700.

44. Once again, both the spirit and some of the language that
can be adduced here as evidence of Richard's ambition are
Shakespeare's, for Cibber has adapted these lines, with addi-
tions, from *3 Henry VI,* indeed from the very speech cited in
note 41. And once again one must note that such lines are not
offered in *Richard III* where they might have been expected. In
the latter play one discovers something closer to malice than to
ambition before Richard's ascendancy, and anxiety afterwards.
"Why, Buckingham, I say I would be king" (IV.ii.12), the terse
prologue to Richard's expression of his desire that the princes in
the Tower be put to death, is accompanied by a gnawing of his
lip and other marks of anger that suggest more fear than pleasure.

45. *Shakespeare's Historical Tragedy of Richard III, Adapted to
Representation by Colley Cibber, as played by Kemble, Cooke and
Kean* (New York: Samuel French, n.d.), p. 3.

46. Cited in *A New Variorum Edition of Shakespeare, The
Tragedy of Richard III,* ed. H. H. Furness, Jr. (Philadelphia: J. B.
Lippincott, 1908), p. 597.

47. Oddly, Macbeth's letter to Lady Macbeth telling her of the
witches' prophecy speaks only "of what greatness is promis'd
thee" (I.vi.12–13). Lady Macbeth, to be sure, speaks at several
points of her husband's ambition:

> Thou wouldst be great,
> Art not without ambition. . . .
> What thou wouldst highly,
> That wouldst thou holily; wouldst not play false,
> And yet wouldst wrongly win. Thou'ldst have, great Glamis,
> That which cries, "Thus thou must do," if thou have it. . . ."
> (I.v.18–23)

On the eve of the murder she reminds him of "the hope . . . Wherein you dress'd yourself," suggests that he would "have that / Which thou esteem'st the ornament of life," and reminds him that he did "break this enterprise to me" (I.vii.35–48). But all of this language, like "the golden round," is hers, and Shakespeare gives us no opportunity to see Macbeth in a moment of unequivocal ambition. He mentions ambition once, when in soliloquy he anticipates the inevitable consequences of the murder and admits that the only "spur / To prick the sides of [his] intent" is "Vaulting ambition, which o'erleaps itself, / And falls on th'other—" (I.vii, 25–27). Imaging ambition as a horse, he sees it as rising only to fall, as self-destructive and doomed to failure. This is hardly like what one normally thinks of as the ambition that incites men to political crime. Even Macbeth's first assertion of a desire for the crown, "the swelling act / Of the imperial theme" (I.iii.128–29), is extraordinarily vague, scarcely focused on the pleasures of being king, and it is followed immediately by lines that seem to express premature remorse for an evil deed not yet even fully imagined. Macbeth mentions the crown again during the "show of Eight Kings and Banquo last," and once again his words suggest guilt and fear rather than an interest in royal power for himself and his descendants: "Thou art too like the spirit of Banquo. Down! / Thy crown does sear mine eyeballs" (IV.i. 112–13).

48. William Davenant, *Macbeth*, II.i.49–50. My text of the 1674 adaptation is Spencer, *Five Restoration Adaptations of Shakespeare*.

49. The curious scene in which Shakespeare's innocent Malcolm "confesses" to crimes of great magnitude, then claims simply to have been testing Macduff, may be Shakespeare's unsuccessful attempt to suggest that Malcolm, in his combination of Duncan-like purity and an imaginative knowledge approximating that which Macbeth learns through unacceptable experience, is the unique exception to the rule, a prince who combines the requisite qualities.

50. See Hazelton Spencer, *Shakespeare Improved* (New York: Frederick Ungar, 1963), pp. 158–59, for some astute observations about Davenant's systematization of *Macbeth* and his accord with Dryden's dictum that "it is not permissible . . . to set up a character as composed of mighty opposites."

51. Cited in Furness, *Variorum Macbeth* (1873), p. 295.

52. See Geoffrey Bullough, *Narrative and Dramatic Sources of Shakespeare*, VII (London: Routledge and Kegan Paul, 1973), pp. 431–32.

53. Ibid., 448–49.

54. Ibid.

55. D. A. Traversi, *An Approach to Shakespeare* (Garden City: Doubleday, 1956; first published 1938), pp. 156–61.

56. See Dennis Biggins, "Sexuality, Witchcraft, and Violence in *Macbeth*," *Shakespeare Studies* VIII (1975), 255–77.

57. In "The Criminal as Tragic Hero," *Shakespeare Survey* 19 (1966), 12–24, Robert B. Heilman wrestles with the problem of a tragic hero who seems to many, as he did to Davenant, the villain of a melodrama. Though Heilman's conclusions do not agree with mine, they are based on similar difficulties with conventional readings of Macbeth's character and its context. The appropriateness of Shakespeare's making a hero of a criminal becomes less problematic when Macbeth's criminality is seen as his tragic predicament, as I have been suggesting it is.

58. For a listing of some of these critics, see p. 26 above.

59. Rolf Soellner, *Timon of Athens, Shakespeare's Pessimistic Tragedy* (Columbus: Ohio State University Press, 1979) attempts gamely but unconvincingly to include *Timon* among the successes.

60. Shadwell's adaptation was first performed in 1678. There is no modern edition.

61. Hazelton Spencer, *Shakespeare Improved*, pp. 286–87.

62. My text of Tate's adaptation of *Coriolanus* is the first edition, London, 1682.

63. Just so Davenant eliminates the obscurity which makes Shakespeare's Macbeth and the treacherous Thane of Cawdor syntactically almost indistinguishable in Ross's account (I.ii.49–59) of their confrontation.

64. Rothstein, *Restoration Tragedy*, p. 152, usefully discusses the "consciousness of hierarchy" that informs heroic plays; Barbeau's opening chapter is useful for describing the rational basis of Restoration tragedy in general as well as for Dryden.

65. See *Shakespeare and the Common Understanding*, pp. 11–28.

66. Heilman, *Tragedy and Melodrama*, p. 16.

67. John Hollander, "Hobbes, 1651," in *Movie-going, and Other Poems* (New York: Atheneum, 1962).

68. On paradox in Renaissance literature see Rosalie Colie, *Paradoxica Epidemica* (Princeton: Princeton University Press, 1966). See Joan Webber, *Contrary Music: The Prose Style of John Donne* (Madison: University of Wisconsin Press, 1963) for a discussion of the "baroque" literary personality which is similar to what I am describing in Renaissance sensibility; see also Grudin, *Mighty Opposites,* for the tracing of some philosophical backgrounds to Renaissance paradoxicality.

69. Thomas S. Kuhn, *The Structure of Scientific Revolutions* (Chicago: University of Chicago Press, 1962).

70. *Preface to Troilus and Cressida,* p. 135.

Chapter 4

1. For a bibliography of such studies of Shakespeare see Thomas F. Van Laan, *Role-Playing in Shakespeare* (Toronto: The University Press, 1978), pp. 253–61, and additional items in the review by Scott Colley, *Shakespeare Studies* XII (1979), p. 368.

2. The two kinds of dramaturgy I have described are excellently distinguished as "presentational," or illusionistic, and "representational," or self-reflexive, by Barbara A. Mowat in *The Dramaturgy of Shakespeare's Romances* (Athens: University of Georgia Press, 1976), pp. 35ff. Mowat is one of the few critics who are equally interested in both strategies and see their relationship as significant; it is not coincidental that she is insistent on the reductiveness of thematic interpretation.

3. "The Argument of Comedy," from *English Institute Essays, 1948,* in Leonard F. Dean, ed., *Shakespeare: Modern Essays in Criticism,* rev. ed. (New York: Oxford University Press, 1967), p. 89.

4. *A Natural Perspective: The Development of Shakespearean Comedy and Romance* (New York: Harcourt, Brace and World, 1965), p. 8. In his introduction to *The Tempest* in the Pelican Shakespeare, Frye seems much more willing to talk about plays as if they have some bearing on the world they imitate.

5. Almost persuasive. But to make his point that the real world isn't one of the play's terms, Frye must do some interesting obscuring: e.g., "The world of Leontes' jealousy does not

exist at all: only the consequences of believing in it exist" (p. 115). All that it means to say that the world of Leontes's jealousy doesn't exist is that Leontes happens to be wrong. In the illusion of the play that jealousy is palpable to Leontes and no more or less existential than Othello's; in "Some Dramatic Techniques in *The Winter's Tale*," *Shakespeare Survey*, 22 (1969), 93–107, William H. Matchett demonstrates that certain hints lead the audience early on to some of Leontes's very suspicions.

6. Frank Kermode, ed., *The Tempest,* The Arden Shakespeare (London: Methuen, 1961; first published 1954), p. liv.

7. Ibid., p. lxxxii. Interestingly, when Kermode discusses the ostentatious observance of the unity of time in *The Tempest,* one of the factors generally seen as calling attention to the fact that the play is a play, he explains the phenomenon entirely in terms of the requirements of the play's action (p. lxxvi).

8. Mowat, *Shakespeare's Romances,* rightly takes me to task (p. 67) for just such a schematization of *Cymbeline* as "a play concerned solely with play-making," a view I now recognize to have been simplistic.

9. An interesting analogy to some of the following remarks is found in the introduction by Hermann Broch to Rachel Bespaloff, *On the Iliad,* Bollingen series IX (New York: Pantheon Books, 1949), particularly Broch's discussion of "the style of old age."

10. Thomas Mann, *The Holy Sinner,* tr. H. T. Lowe-Porter (New York: Alfred A. Knopf, 1951), p. 94.

11. P. 98. Significantly, "The Bad Children" is the title of the chapter that recounts the initial incest, and thus the phrase calls attention to Clemen's narrative.

12. "But to [the Pope's] blood the identity of wife and mother was familiar long before he learned the truth and play-acted about it" (p. 330). In the German text: "lange bevor er die Wahrheit erfuhr und sich gar komödiantisch darüber entsetzte" (*Der Erwählte* [Frankfurt: S. Fischer Verlag, 1961], p. 314).

13. P. 332. In the German, p. 316:

"Und hat, lose Frau, nur Euer Spiel mit Uns getrieben?"
"Da Ihr Euer Spiel mit mir treiben wolltet—"
"Wir gedachten, Gott eine Unterhaltung damit zu bieten."
"Dabei ging ich Euch gern zur Hand. Und doch war es kein Spiel."

14. Mowat, *Shakespeare's Romances* (p. 5), quotes Herbert McArthur, "Tragic and Comic Modes," *Criticism* 3 (1961), 45: "The indefinably odd quality which some commentators have found in the 'late comedies' may perhaps be attributed to Shakespeare's placing events ordinarily suggestive of the tragic mode into the framework of a closed system, the domain of the comic spirit. Was he trying to write tragedy from God's viewpoint, instead of from man's?"

15. *The Winter's Tale,* I.ii.187–89; III.ii.35–37, 28–29; V.ii. 79–81; V.iii.151–55.

16. *Confessions of Felix Krull, Confidence Man,* tr. Denver Lindley (New York: Alfred A. Knopf, 1955), p. 253.

17. Pp. 20–21; cf. the episode of the circus and Felix's comments on it, pp. 189–95.

18. For a set of interesting essays that will suggest how many other kinds of things are going on in these plays, see Carol McGinnis Kay and Henry E. Jacobs, eds., *Shakespeare's Romances Reconsidered* (Lincoln: University of Nebraska Press, 1979). See also Charles Frey, "Interpreting *The Winter's Tale,*" *SEL* 18 (1978), 207–29; C. L. Barber, " 'Thou that beget'st him that did thee beget': Transformation in *Pericles* and *The Winter's Tale,*" *Shakespeare Survey* 22 (1969), 59–67; Murray M. Schwartz, "Between Fantasy and Imagination: A Psychological Exploration of *Cymbeline,*" in Frederick Crews, ed., *Psychoanalysis and Literary Process* (Cambridge, Ma.: Winthrop Publishers, 1970), pp. 219–83. These essays are virtually a random sampling, representative in their variety (and their tilt towards psychoanalytic methodology) of recent excellent work on the last plays.

19. *Shakespeare and the Common Understanding,* pp. 192–237.

20. *Joseph and His Brothers,* tr. H. T. Lowe-Porter (New York: Alfred A. Knopf, 1948), p. 235.

21. *The Black Swan,* tr. Willard R. Trask (New York: Alfred A. Knopf, 1954), p. 133.

22. *The Winter's Tale,* III.ii.81.

Index

Index